High Protein, Low GI, BOLD FLAVOR

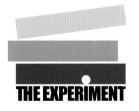

THE EXPERIMENT

BECAUSE EVERY BOOK IS A TEST OF NEW IDEAS

Quinoa, Roasted Sweet Potato and Pomegranate (page 150)

High Protein, Low GI, BOLD FLAVOR

RECIPES TO BOOST HEALTH AND PROMOTE WEIGHT LOSS

FIONA CARNS

THE EXPERIMENT

NEW YORK

High Protein, Low GI, Bold Flavor: Recipes to Boost Health and Promote Weight Loss

The Experiment, LLC
260 Fifth Avenue
New York, NY 10001–6408
www.theexperimentpublishing.com

Note: This is a cookbook, not a diet book. If you or one of your family members has a pre-existing health condition, are on medication, and/or have specific dietary requirements, you should consult your doctor, dietitian, or specialist prior to significantly changing your diet. Nuts feature strongly in many of these recipes.

The Experiment's books are available at special discounts when purchased in bulk for premiums and sales promotions as well as for fundraising or educational use. For details, contact us at info@theexperimentpublishing.com.

Library of Congress Control Number: 2011938431
ISBN 978-1-61519-037-9
Ebook ISBN 978-1-61519-137-6

Cover design by Susi Oberhelman
Cover photographs by Simon Griffiths
Author photograph by Andrew Sawenko
Food styling by Fiona Hammond
Text design by Pauline Neuwirth, Neuwirth & Associates, Inc.

Manufactured in China
Distributed in the United States by Workman Publishing Company, Inc.
Distributed simultaneously in Canada by Thomas Allen & Son Ltd.
First published January 2012
10 9 8 7 6 5 4 3 2 1

To my amazing husband, Greg, for his unflagging encouragement and support, and to my beautiful friend Pix, who has shown me that there are no hurdles that can't be overcome

Contents

Foreword

When Fiona Carns wrote this cookbook, little did she realize that it was at the cutting edge of medicine. One of the biggest and best diet trials ever done has just proven that a *combination* high-protein *and* low-GI diet improves the ability to sustain weight loss and is superior to either a high-protein or low-GI diet alone. The combined diet was not only effective for maintaining weight loss; it had the lowest dropout rate (that is, the highest acceptability) of the five diets that were compared. And the good news doesn't end there: The high-protein, low-GI diet reduced one of the most reliable indicators of heart disease risk. So with this book, Fiona Carns brings you the best of both worlds—the flavor and enjoyment of good food *and* the knowledge that you are doing the best for your body.

—Dr. Jennie Brand-Miller,
author of *The New Glucose Revolution*
and *The Low GI Handbook*
September 2011

Introduction

I'm now entering my eighth year of embracing a lean-protein and low-glycemic-index (low-GI) lifestyle, and I love it. Maintaining this regimen has not been a matter of discipline but rather of understanding what makes me feel and look good, while still satisfying my need for great-tasting, nutritious food. In conjunction with regular exercise, my weight has stayed constant and my motivation has remained strong.

When I decided to change my diet in 1999, I had been unable to shed the extra weight I was carrying after the birth of my third child, despite regular exercise and an extremely low-fat diet. I ate very little butter or oil, no avocados, nuts, or seeds, the occasional piece of red meat, and only a sprinkling of cheese. Low fat was my focus, with little regard for the nutritional value of my food. Eating any fat makes you fat, or so I thought. The prospect of increasing my protein and reducing my carbohydrates while enjoying the good fats seemed very attractive and manageable, and by then I was keen to try a new approach.

My first few months were fairly strict: no pasta, rice, potatoes, bread, or sugar, of course, no processed refined carbs, limited fruit (I ate mostly berries and stone fruits), and no beans or legumes. Lean protein ruled the day, with an abundance of low-GI vegetables. Saturated fats continued to be a stranger to my world, but the good fats (nuts, avocados, and olive oil) became main players.

My weight loss was steady, and with it came a terrific sense of well-being. I no longer suffered from fluctuating energy levels, bloating, and frequent indigestion—things I had commonly experienced after a low-fat, low-protein, high-carb meal. Suddenly, I was full of energy and ready for anything.

In 2002 I wrote *Low Carbohydrate High Flavor Recipes,* a book of simple meals that kept me in my low-carb zone. Since then, my eating regimen has expanded to include more low-GI carbs—the smart carbs that make you feel full for longer.

My concern for the rapid increase in obesity and type 2 diabetes and my passion for healthy cooking have inspired me to create this new collection of recipes. It caters to all members of the family (and I know from experience that some can be fussier than others!), using nutritiously dense foods that offer plenty of protein and are low GI. The recipes are simple and healthy, with a focus on real unprocessed food: fish, poultry, lean pork and veal, a little red meat, eggs, low-GI vegetables and fruit, legumes, nuts and seeds, low-fat dairy products, and all the good fats. They are filled with flavor, so you can enjoy your mealtimes without feeling for a minute that you are missing out on anything. Welcome to the world of low GI. Just by making a few simple changes to your diet, you will increase your energy levels, assist in lowering blood cholesterol, and reduce your risk of heart disease, diabetes, and even some forms of cancer, while achieving and maintaining your ideal body weight. Here is the road to optimum health. Enjoy!

Foods to Eat on a High-Protein, Low-GI Regimen

Since writing my first book, my recipes have developed to include more low-GI carbohydrates and techniques on how to lower the GI of a meal; although in some cases this means increasing the amount of carbohydrates, I use low-GI carbohydrates—the "smart carbs."

There are no hard-and-fast rules for the exact ratio of protein, carbohydrates, and fat in each meal. Generally, lean protein is the heart of the meal, accompanied by low-GI vegetables, fruits, and legumes, a splash of low-fat dairy products, and the good unsaturated fats. As we know, carbohydrates and fat are used for energy, and protein for cell repair and construction. By reducing the carbohydrates and fat in your diet, you allow your body to access your fat reserves. Put this together with the benefits of eating low-GI carbs (giving you more control over your blood sugars, fat storage, appetite, and energy levels) and you have a successful regimen for weight loss and for maintaining a healthy weight. The recipes in this book embrace these principles without the need for tedious weighing and counting.

The GI ranking system has been established through complex tests using real food and real people. In a nutshell, a GI below 55 is low, 55 through 70 is intermediate, and above 70 is high. Although different research bodies perform these tests and establish rankings, an international standard for GI testing was established in 2010. In Australia, a "GI" symbol, developed by the Sydney University Glycaemic Index Research Institute (which counts Olympic gold medalist Ian Thorpe as a spokesperson) and endorsed by Diabetes Australia, is found on many low-GI products on supermarket shelves. The United States and Canada do not have such a widely adopted GI symbol program, though a "GI tested" service mark has been introduced by Toronto's Glycemic Index Laboratories, and other testing entities also provide low-GI certification for packaged foods.

Education is the key to success. With a basic understanding of the simple nutritional principles of food, the concept behind high-protein, low-GI eating will become clearer.

What follows is a brief discussion of protein, carbohydrates, and fat, and a chart that shows you which foods to enjoy, limit, and avoid. Obviously, this is a guide only and is by no means conclusive.

PROTEIN

Protein is essential for the overall health of our bodies, controlling the building and repair of every living cell, including tissues of the brain, muscles, and blood, and regulating our immune system and organ function.

Animal proteins (red and white meat, fish, and eggs) are complete proteins, as they contain all of the essential amino acids. Tofu is also an excellent source of protein. Other plant proteins do not contain all of the essential amino acids and are considered incomplete. These include beans and legumes, nuts and seeds, grains, and products made from these foods. The meat proteins used in my recipes are predominantly trimmed of excess fat, and with any slow-cooked dishes I recommend skimming the fat off the top before serving.

CARBOHYDRATES

Carbohydrates are divided into two categories, based on their chemical structure: simple and complex. Simple carbohydrates (now sometimes referred to broadly as "sugars") include sugar, honey, maple syrup, fruit (fructose), and dairy products (lactose). Complex carbohydrates (now sometimes referred to broadly as "starches") include fiber and starchy foods, such as potatoes, pasta, legumes, whole grains, and bread. This division, however, does not take into account how the body digests them. It is now widely known that, like fats, not all carbohydrates are the same, and the body metabolizes them differently.

When we eat carbohydrates, our body breaks them down into glucose, which causes our blood sugar levels to rise. To control this rise and lower our sugar levels, our body produces insulin—the facilitator in fat storage and an appetite stimulant. The greater the amount and the more refined the carbohydrate, the higher and faster the insulin response. This seesawing not only causes hunger but can also cause exhaustion. Low-GI carbohydrates are absorbed slowly into the bloodstream, resulting in slow glucose release and a slower, more controlled production of insulin. This in turn results in sustained energy levels and a sense of feeling fuller longer. In basic terms, the GI is the rate at which the body digests carbohydrates. The lower the index, the more slowly the carbohydrate is digested.

FATS

Fats are a great source of energy and are vital for many of the body's functions, including the transportation and absorption of vitamins, assisting with the immune system, and regulating our hormones. There are several types of fats, containing very different properties. Monounsaturated fats are found in oils such as olive oil, rice bran oil, and peanut oil, and in nuts and seeds. Seen as "good fats," these fats reduce levels of "bad cholesterol" (or LDL) and raise "good cholesterol" (or HDL) in our blood.

Many of the fats in a low-GI diet are found in protein-based foods such as fish, green leafy vegetables, and seeds such as flaxseeds, sesame seeds, and pumpkin seeds. The essential fatty acids are part of the polyunsaturated fat group. They are essential for good health and, unlike other fats, cannot be made by the body. Not only do these fats protect against heart disease and stroke, they lower blood fat levels and are essential in regulating the immune, digestive, and reproductive systems.

Saturated fats are found in dairy products, eggs, and meat. High consumption of these products can result in increased blood cholesterol and blood fat levels. When it comes to dairy products, you can choose between full-fat, reduced-fat, and low-fat products—your decision should be based on taste, quality, and quantity used. Often when fat is removed from food products, carbohydrates are added in the form of sugar, which not only affects the taste but also increases the GI. Eating low fat does not necessarily mean that you are consuming fewer calories, nor does it mean the product is better for you. Read the labels carefully and let common sense be your guide.

Trans fats, also known as trans-fatty acids, are the worst fats and the ones to avoid at all cost—they are highly toxic and offer no benefits. Like saturated fats, they will increase your LDL and lower your HDL, thereby increasing your risk of heart disease. These fats are found in some animal foods and are man-made through the partial hydrogenation of oils. Many packaged cookies, crackers, margarines, and snack foods once contained trans fats, but many manufacturers have revamped their recipes to eliminate all or most of the trans fats.

Fast foods and highly processed packaged carbs such as cakes and cookies don't rate a mention here, as they are high in fat and often contain dangerous trans-fatty acids. All the grains and pastas listed are low or medium GI but I *have* limited their use to side dishes rather than having them as the main component of a meal, leaving room for you to include lean protein and an abundance of vegetables.

GOLDEN RULES FOR MAINTAINING A HIGH-PROTEIN, LOW-GI LIFESTYLE

- Choose small amounts of low-GI carbohydrates—that is, the smart carbs that are absorbed slowly into the blood, meaning slow glucose release and sustained energy levels. Generally speaking, the higher the fiber and the more unrefined the carbohydrate, the lower the GI.
- You can include medium- or high-GI carbohydrates in your diet in moderation, as there are ways to reduce their GI. The simplest way to do this is to add an acid, such as lemon juice or vinegar, and a little good unsaturated fat, and combine it with a low-GI carbohydrate.
- Include protein in every meal and snack—it lowers the GI of the accompanying carbs and satisfies your appetite.
- Don't overeat. This is so easy to do when you're enjoying a meal, even if it is high protein, low GI, and low fat. Keep an eye on portion size—to maintain a healthy weight, you must balance the energy you take in with the energy you expend.
- Drink plenty of water. It is vital for digestion and the transportation of nutrients and minerals throughout your body to enable normal bodily function. It also prevents constipation, is essential in fat burning and the elimination of toxins, and controls the body's temperature. The basic recommendation for optimum health is to drink eight to ten glasses a

day—more with warmer weather and exercise. Remember, thirst is often mistaken for hunger, so drink up!

- There is a tendency for vegetables to stick while pan-frying, so instead of adding more oil, simply add a little stock or water and reduce the heat. Covering the pan will steam the food—this technique is particularly useful when cooking egg dishes, as the base often cooks well before the top.

	ENJOY	LIMIT	AVOID
Meat, Seafood and Other Protein	chicken and turkey (both white and dark meat; avoid the skin), lobster, mackerel, oysters, shrimp, salmon, tuna, whiting, tofu, protein powder	lean cuts of beef and lamb, lean bacon, ham, pancetta, and prosciutto	any canned or processed product with added sugar
Eggs and Dairy Products	eggs (to lower fat intake, use a combination of egg whites and fewer yolks in omelettes and frittatas), low-fat cottage cheese, low-fat milk or yogurt	low-fat feta, mozzarella, ricotta, and cheddar cheese, full-fat Parmesan and goat cheese, whole-milk yogurt	whole milk, heavy cream
Nuts and Seeds	unsalted raw pumpkin, sesame, and sunflower seeds	raw or roasted nuts and seeds (a handful a day is a good rule of thumb), nut oils	any type of fried nuts, with or without sugar
	ENJOY—LOW GI (below 55)	**LIMIT—INTERMEDIATE GI (55 to 70)**	**AVOID—HIGH GI (above 70)**
Vegetables and Herbs	asparagus, bok choy, broccoli, broccolini, Brussels sprouts, cabbage (red, green, Chinese), carrots, cauliflower, celeriac, celery, choy sum, cucumbers, eggplant, fennel, green beans, herbs (basil, cilantro, mint, parsley, tarragon, thyme), Jerusalem artichokes, lettuce (Boston, green leaf, iceberg, red leaf, red oak), mushrooms, onions (red, spring, yellow, white), parsnips, peas (green, snow, sugar snap), radishes, rutabagas, salad greens (chicory, arugula, endive, mixed), spinach, squash, sweet corn, sweet potatoes, Swiss chard, tomatoes, turnips, zucchini	beets, pumpkin	broad (fava) beans, white potatoes
Fruits	apples, apricots, bananas, blackberries, blueberries, fresh figs, currants, dates, grapes, kiwi fruit, lemons, limes, mandarin oranges, nectarines, oranges, passionfruit, peaches, pears, pineapple (fresh or canned in fruit juice), plums, raspberries, strawberries, raisins	honeydew melon, watermelon, mangos, canteloupe, dried figs, dried dates	lychees, canned fruit with added sugars or in syrup
Legumes	butter (lima) beans, cannellini beans, chickpeas, great northern beans, lentils, red kidney beans, soybeans (edamame), split peas		
Grains and Grain Products	barley (pearl), buckwheat, bulgur (cracked wheat), freekeh (cracked green wheat), old-fashioned rolled oats, quinoa, durum wheat pasta, whole grain pasta, spaghetti, spirali, rice noodles, cellophane (bean thread) noodles, soba (buckwheat) noodles, long-grain white or brown rice, whole grain high-fiber breads, whole grain breads with seeds or nuts	couscous, polenta, egg noodles, orecchiette, rigatoni, basmati rice, wild rice, English muffins, pita bread, light rye bread	corn pasta, rice pasta, glutinous (sticky) white rice, jasmine rice, white or brown instant rice (except brands that specify "low-GI"), white bread, dark rye bread, any highly processed bread or cereal with added sugars

≡ Open Steak Sandwich with Caramelized Onions and Goat Cheese (page 132)

High Protein, Low GI, Bold Flavor

Kids and Family

High-protein, low-GI cooking for you and your family is easy with a few simple changes. It's true, you can lead your children to the dinner plate but you can't make them eat; however, by setting an example from an early age, you can help form a healthy approach to eating that (hopefully) will stay with them for life.

Most kids love white—white bread, white short-grain rice, white pasta, and white potatoes (mashed potatoes and potato chips in particular). These things are not completely off the menu, but could perhaps do with some tweaking: Try some low-GI, high-fiber whole grain bread or even low-GI white bread from your local bakery as a starting point. Change over to basmati rice, and cook sweet potatoes instead of white potatoes—see also the Sides chapter (page 135) for a variety of vegetable dishes that will delight young palates. Serve a small portion of thick pasta as a side, not as the main part of a dish. My kids love pasta and noodles, and while they are high in carbohydrates, durum wheat pasta and some noodles are low GI. A number of my recipes suggest rigatoni, farfalle, or orecchiette as the side dish. I must say, I prefer beans and legumes instead of pasta—as these foods are full of fiber, vitamins, and minerals and are lower in carbohydrates—but unless you want to cook separate meals every day, a little compromise is required!

When buying ingredients for your family meals, keep the words "low interference" firmly in mind. You want whole foods that are as unrefined and unprocessed as possible. Think fiber and density (not aerated) and as raw and natural as you can find. Choose food without added sugar, starch, or artificial flavorings or colorings. Encourage your children to try different foods, no matter how taxing it may seem. Spark their interest by inviting them to participate in the preparation and cooking of meals.

Snacks are a great way to introduce new foods and eating habits to your family. Children's motors are different from adults', as they are still growing (although many adults continue to grow horizontally), and so they need a constant supply of fuel. Try some of these child-friendly low-GI snacks:

- a piece of low-GI fruit, such as apples, stone fruit, or citrus, or a bowl of berries
- a protein shake with fruit and yogurt (page 24)
- a toasted low-GI bread sandwich, pita pocket, or wrap with either shredded turkey, ham, canned salmon, or tuna with low-fat cheese and vegetables, such as lettuce and tomato
- low-GI crackers, carrots, snow peas, endive leaves, baby romaine leaves or celery sticks with hummus, tzatziki, or a homemade tuna dip, made with canned tuna, cottage cheese, low-fat cream cheese, lemon juice, salt and pepper (finely chopped celery or cucumber may also be added to the dip)
- a handful of nuts and low-GI dried fruit
- skewers of frozen mango and banana (not overripe)

It may seem ridiculous to include something as simple as an apple in this list, but statistics show that our children are still not eating enough fruit—particularly young teenagers. Vegetables are another problem, with few eating the required five to seven servings per day. It's easy to stick to the same old routine—spaghetti on Monday night, pork chops and mashed potatoes on Tuesday—but this may lead to a lazy palate. I urge you to keep trying different recipes full of lean, heart-smart protein, low-GI vegetables and fruit, low-fat dairy, beans and legumes, nuts and seeds. Of course, this can mean more work at the end of an already-busy day, and often involves heartbreak, as your loved ones wrinkle their noses and refuse to try a second bite. More often than not, this reaction stems from ignorance or an unwillingness to accept something unfamiliar. Persist, I say! Take a deep breath and say, "Just try it."

High Protein, Low GI, Bold Flavor

The High-Protein, Low-GI Kitchen

Like many people, I prefer to cook with fresh produce, but today's hectic pace prevents me from visiting the markets and grocery stores every day. Thankfully, there are some excellent canned and frozen products available that have been picked at their prime and snap-frozen or packaged, retaining valuable vitamins and minerals.

A word of warning: As with low-fat, there are new low-carb and low-GI items hitting the supermarket shelves daily. The low-GI endorsements on packaged food do not necessarily mean the food is good for you and can be consumed with abandon. Similarly, the fact that one brand is labeled "low carb" or "low GI" does not automatically make it superior to another brand that makes no mention of the glycemc index or carbohydrate content.

Compare the nutritional information on the packages and make your own informed decision. For a comprehensive listing of accredited GI values for a wide range of foods, consult the most current annual edition of The Low GI Shopper's Guide to GI Values by Dr. Jennie Brand-Miller and Kaye Foster-Powell.

Be aware too that the flavor of these low-GI/carb/fat products may have been altered for the worse. I have learned this the hard way, and many of the products I use may not be the lowest in carbohydrates on the shelves and may maintain a small amount of sugars. I base my decision on taste, quality, and how natural the products are.

Below is a list of foods I use regularly. Of course, these are only suggestions and you should feel free to make your own choices. Check the shelves regularly, as new and exciting products are being released all the time.

Almonds
Packed with protein and fiber, almonds taste great in muesli and salads or as a snack on their own. Ground almonds (also sold as almond meal) are useful as a thickener for sauces and curries and as a binder for meatballs, and they add a crunchy crust to fish fillets, chicken, or fruit desserts.

Amaranth
An ancient high-protein cereal, amaranth is full of essential amino acids, particularly lysine, which most grains lack. Gluten free and high in fiber, it is a great addition to your breakfast. Amaranth is available at supermarkets and natural food stores.

Anchovies
Small silver fish in the herring family, anchovies are high in omega-3 fats. Their pungent flavor adds depth to salads and sauces.

Artichoke Hearts
Artichokes are low in calories and high in fiber, and convenient if you buy them jarred, canned, or frozen. Marinated artichoke hearts make a good choice for salads, antipasto platters, and slow-cooked chicken dishes—a little goes a long way.

Bacon
Bacon, prosciutto, pancetta, and ham are all cured meats, and although they are excellent sources of B vitamins and protein, they are also very high in salt and contain nitrites as a preservative. When shopping, look for natural products trimmed of excess fats, and enjoy them in moderate amounts.

Balsamic Vinegar
I use aged balsamic vinegar in many of my dressings and marinades for its complex, slightly sweet flavor. Apple balsamic vinegar, made from cooked apple juice aged in a succession of wooden barrels (in the same manner as balsamic vinegar) is

delicious and worth seeking out. You can approximate its flavor by combining equal amounts of balsamic vinegar and apple juice concentrate. Orange-flavored balsamic is also available.

Beans

I prefer to soak dried beans overnight and then cook them in stock, but canned beans are a real time-saver. Organic brands are generally lower in sodium than conventional brands; rinsing canned beans before use further reduces the sodium.

Beets

While fresh beets are the best choice (and only take minutes to steam or microwave), canned and pickled beets add quick color, flavor, and nutrients to weeknight dinners and salads. Check the sodium levels on the package when choosing a brand.

Berries

Buy fresh blueberries, raspberries, blackberries, or mixed berries when they're in season. Otherwise, try the frozen varieties by Wyman's or Dole.

Bread

Look for breads made from whole grains (these should be first in the list of ingredients) and no added sugars. Dense, solid loaves that include seeds and dried fruit are generally higher in fiber, which in turn lowers the GI of the bread.

Capers

My favorite capers are the dry salted ones, but they must be washed well before use. If unavailable, there are several good alternatives: Look for capers in vinegar or white wine vinegar. Small, or nonpareil, capers are best for cooking; the larger capers have a less intense flavor and are great with antipasto and cheese platters.

Cheese

Some low-fat cheeses are better than others. I use low- or reduced-fat ricotta, cottage cheese, cream cheese, and cheddar cheese with great success. For goat cheese and Parmesan, I stick to the full-fat version but use limited quantities. A small amount of flavorful cheese can make a big impact in a dish.

Chicken

To avoid repetition I do not state this at every mention in the recipes, but I always use organic chickens (or if I'm stuck, free-range). The flavor is far superior, and the chicken is free from pesticides, antibiotics, and hormones.

Chocolate

Not only do darker chocolates contain less sugar than milk chocolate, but they have more cocoa, which is a rich source of antioxidants. Dark, extra-fine chocolate by Lindt with 70 percent cocoa is perfect for that sweet occasion—a little shaved over your dessert goes a long way. Also available in a variety of flavors, including chile, orange, and almond, although the cocoa percentage is lower with these.

Coconut Milk

Make sure you buy coconut milk, not coconut cream (which is sweetened and thick). I use low-fat coconut milk, often labeled as "lite."

Crispbreads

Crispbreads make an excellent bread or toast substitute when you need a base or a little crunch. Ryvita makes oat crispbreads with sesame seeds and pumpkin seeds, both of which are low GI.

Dressings

Newman's Own salad dressings are made from all-natural ingredients. Generally I prefer to make my own dressing, even if it's just a simple combination of extra virgin olive oil, balsamic or white wine vinegar, and a good squeeze of citrus. Not only does it taste fresher, the acid reduces the GI of your meal!

Eggs

I prefer to buy organic eggs, although I will settle for free-range eggs if organic ones are unavailable. Organic eggs contain fewer toxins, and both organic and free-range farming techniques are more humane than the average chicken farm. Several suppliers now produce eggs enhanced with omega-3 fats, which is a worthwhile bonus.

Evaporated Milk

Nestlé's Carnation light and creamy evaporated milk is a great alternative to cream (although it can't be whipped). It has a rich, full flavor with 95 percent less fat than regular cream.

Freekeh

A natural grain from a green wheat, freekeh is available cracked or as a whole grain. It is very high in fiber and low GI. Use it as a side dish in the same way you would serve quinoa, rice, or pasta.

Fruits and Vegetables

Buy fresh fruits and vegetables when you can, making the most of what is in season. Frozen, canned, or packaged foods are okay when you are caught short, as long as there are no added sugars. The shorter the list of additives on the label, the better. Unless specified, all fruits and vegetables in the recipes are medium sized.

Herbs

Store fresh herbs with their roots in a glass of water. Cover the herbs and glass with a plastic bag and refrigerate, changing the water daily. They should last for up to a week. Beware of bottled or tube varieties—the flavor is ordinary, and they are often loaded with sugar. I use generous amounts of fresh herbs in my recipes; they contribute so much flavor while adding practically nothing in the way of calories or carbs.

Horseradish Sauce

Bottled horseradish can't beat fresh, but there's no denying its convenience, or the zip it can add to foods. Look for a brand with no added sugars and minimal preservatives.

Jams

The best jam or fruit spread is all fruit, sweetened only with fruit juice concentrate. Check natural food stores for a good selection of jams and preserves.

Lentils

As far as dried lentils go, my favorite kind are *lentilles de Puy*, or French green lentils: They have a thinner skin than most lentils, are higher in magnesium and iron, and are lower in carbs. They are available in most good natural food stores and supermarkets. Canned lentils are generally not as good as those you cook yourself but are convenient for a quick soup or salad.

LSA

The acronym LSA stands for linseed (flaxseed), sunflower seeds, and almonds, and LSA is sold as a preground mixture in natural food stores in Australia. You can easily make your own by processing equal quantities of these three foods until finely ground; make sure to store the mixture in an airtight container in the fridge. LSA can be used in smoothies and sprinkled on cereal.

Olive Oil

I use cold-pressed extra virgin olive oil in salads and as a finishing touch to many warm dishes. Cold-pressed olive oil is loaded with enzymes, nutrients, and antioxidants and is also an excellent source of monounsaturated fats. Colavita produces a range of cold-pressed extra virgin olive oil, including basil and lemon flavors. Olive oil spray by Bertolli (available natural and with garlic) is also a good buy.

Pappadums

With just over 1 gram carbohydrate per piece, pappadums are great accessories to soups, salads, and curries. Cook them in the microwave and avoid the excess saturated fat that comes from frying.

Pomegranate Molasses

This is the concentrated juice of pomegranates and is used as a sweet-and-sour flavor enhancer in Middle Eastern cooking. Look for it in the international aisle of better-stocked supermarkets or in specialty food stores. If you can't find it, you can make a close approximation by simmering ¼ cup pomegranate or ruby red grapefruit juice with 2 tablespoons maple syrup and 2 tablespoons lime or lemon juice until the mixture is reduced to 6 tablespoons.

Protein Powder

There are many different brands on the market with varying nutritional qualities. Choose vanilla protein powder with natural ingredients—no artificial sweeteners, flavors, or preservatives. Look for a brand that contains whey isolate, which is higher in protein than whey concentrate. Check the directions for use, as the recommended quantities can vary from brand to brand. Protein powder is available at natural food stores and some drugstores.

Quinoa

This ancient grain is packed with essential nutrients and is high in protein, iron, and calcium. Like freekeh, it may be used in place of rice or pasta. It is most commonly available as cream-colored grains, but it also comes in red and black varieties.

Salmon

This popular cold-water fish is an excellent source of both protein and omega-3 fats. Whether you buy it smoked or fresh, wild salmon is the healthiest choice, though farmed salmon is more prevalent. Canned salmon is, luckily, all wild-caught.

Salt

I love the texture and taste of sea salt—it is expensive, but the intense flavor generally means you don't have to use as much. When I cook, I use Maldon Sea Salt Flakes, a completely natural product with a wonderful flavor. I crumble the flakes with my fingers as I add them to food. Fine sea salt can be used instead. Because sea salt contains little to no iodine (important to proper thyroid function), it's a good idea to also keep iodized table salt on hand to use in cooking and baking. Lite Salt, a low-sodium salt, is a good alternative to regular salt.

Sambal Oelek

This spicy condiment, made from red chiles and vinegar, is perfect in curries, marinades, and slow-cooked dishes when you want to add a little heat. It is available at Asian markets and in the international aisle of larger supermarkets; look for a brand without added sugar.

Sardines

Sardines are very high in omega-3 fats and, if you buy them whole, calcium. Because they are so far down on the food chain, sardines contain little to no mercury, making them a smart seafood choice.

Sauerkraut

A cool, crunchy, and flavorful side dish, sauerkraut is made from nutritious, high-fiber cabbage. It is so low in carbs that it has no GI ranking. Unpasteurized sauerkraut, found in the refrigerated section of natural food stores, offers the added benefit of probiotics.

Shallots

Fried shallots are great as a garnish on Asian dishes. They are available in some specialty stores, but if you can't find them you can easily make your own: Heat ¼ cup olive oil in a small frying pan over medium-high heat. Add 2 to 3 finely sliced shallots (about ½ cup) and a pinch of salt. Cook, stirring, for 2 to 3 minutes until the shallots are lightly golden. Transfer to a plate lined with paper towels to drain. Makes enough for a garnish for 4 people.

Soy Milk

There is a wide range of soy milks available, both refrigerated and in aseptic containers. When shopping, read the packages carefully to ensure you are getting a plain, unsweetened variety. Check the nutrition label and choose a soy milk with less than 10 grams of sugar per serving.

Soy Sauce
See tamari.

Stock

Homemade stock is best. When you are caught short, there are a few good commercial products available in supermarkets, such as Swanson's and College Inn. Beware of the salt content; you may need to dilute the stock with a little water. (Salt-reduced stocks are simply watered-down regular stock, so buy the original and dilute it yourself.) Unless I'm really stuck, I don't use bouillon cubes.

Sunflower and Sesame Seeds

These tiny powerhouses add antioxidants and minerals, as well as crunch and flavor, to salads and vegetables. For extra flavor, you can toast sesame seeds in a dry skillet until lightly colored; sunflower seeds are available dry-roasted in tamari.

Sweeteners

Occasionally I need to add a little sweetness to a dish, and when I do I try to use natural sweeteners with some nutritional value—particularly maple syrup, honey, and apple and pear juice concentrates.

Tamari

A wheat-free soy sauce, tamari has a deep flavor without the strong salty taste of regular soy sauce. San-J makes organic and reduced-sodium varieties. If you can't find tamari, use low-sodium soy sauce.

Tomatoes

Although nothing beats an in-season tomato for flavor, for the rest of the year, canned tomatoes deliver more consistent quality than fresh. Bionaturae sells a line of organic tomato products in cans and jars. I avoid canned products with acetic acid, as I find it adds a slightly metallic taste. Many canned tomato products are high in sodium. Check the labels and purchase products with no salt added if sodium is a concern; you can always adjust the seasonings to suit your taste.

Tomato Ketchup

Regular ketchup is high in both sugar and sodium; however, Heinz makes a good reduced-sugar ketchup.

Tomato Passata

This sieved tomato sauce is smoother and thicker than tomato juice but thinner than paste. Tomato passata is available online and in some stores (Cento is one brand), but if you can't find it you can use tomato sauce or process whole canned tomatoes in juice until smooth.

Tuna

Canned tuna is an absolute must in my pantry. I prefer tuna packed in olive oil and avoid varieties packed in soybean or other types of oil. If the oily taste is not to your liking, you can rinse the tuna before using it or purchase tuna packed in water. Because tuna harbors more mercury than smaller varieties of fish, use common sense and enjoy it as an occasional meal.

Tzatziki

This creamy sauce can be served as a dip with vegetable crudités and complements any curry dish, as well as lamb. You can buy tzatziki in jars or make your own by mixing together 1 cup low-fat plain Greek-style yogurt, 1 tablespoon lemon juice, 1/3 cup grated carrot or cucumber, 1 clove finely chopped garlic, and a pinch each of salt and black pepper.

Vegetables

see fruits and vegetables

Verjuice

A condiment made from unfermented white grapes, verjuice can be used instead of lemon juice or vinegar but has a milder, more subtle flavor. If you can't find it, white wine makes an acceptable substitute.

Vincotto

Made from cooked grape must, this rich and smooth vinegar has no added sugar, no fat, and only 2 grams carbohydrate per tablespoon. It's available at specialty stores and larger supermarkets in a wide range of flavors. It's not cheap, but a little goes a long way.

Yogurt

Yogurt is great with your muesli and fruit for breakfast, dolloped over curries, chicken, or lamb, with any Indian or Moroccan flavored dish, and of course in homemade tzatziki. You may choose to eat reduced-fat yogurt or the full-fat kind in smaller amounts. Whatever your preference, look for a yogurt with no more than 10 grams of sugar per serving. Greek-style yogurts are strained to remove moisture, making them thicker—and higher in protein—than regular yogurt.

A NOTE ABOUT THE NUTRIENT DATA THAT ACCOMPANIES EACH RECIPE: Per-serving nutrient data is provided for calories; grams of protein, carbohydrate, fat, saturated fat, and fiber, and milligrams of cholesterol and sodium. Optional ingredients are not included in the nutrient analysis, nor are spices and black pepper (given their negligible nutrient content). When a recipe provides a range for the quantity of a particular ingredient, the lower amount is used, and the lower number is also used when there is a range of servings.

Breakfasts and Light Lunches

As we all know, breakfast is the most important meal of the day, and these delicious, nutritious recipes will sustain you through the morning. Just remember, if you are adding toast to your meal, make sure it's just one slice of low-GI bread. Many of the fish- and egg-based recipes also make a lovely light lunch, served with a fresh green salad.

Oat and Nut Muesli with Cinnamon and Orange Zest

SERVES 6
Prep time: 10 minutes
Cooking time: 10 minutes

2 cups old-fashioned oats
Grated zest of 2 oranges
¼ cup orange juice
½ cup unsweetened shredded coconut
1 teaspoon ground cinnamon
3 tablespoons slivered almonds, plus
    extra to garnish
3 tablespoons sunflower seeds
3 tablespoons pumpkin seeds
3 tablespoons sesame seeds
3 tablespoons buckwheat
3 tablespoons flaxseeds
3 tablespoons amaranth puffs
1 cup dried currants, chopped dried
    apricots, or dried cranberries (or a
    combination)
3 apples, grated, optional
Blueberries, optional

331 calories; 11 g protein; 47 g carb; 13 g
fat; 2 g saturated fat; 0 mg cholesterol; 10 g
fiber; 9 mg sodium

Traditional Swiss muesli is packed with dried fruit and therefore carbs. To reduce the carb levels and GI rating in this recipe without sacrificing flavor, I have used nuts, seeds, and low-GI fruit, such as dried currants, apricots, and cranberries.

Preheat the oven to 400°F and line a large rimmed baking sheet with parchment paper.

Place the oats in a line on the prepared sheet and sprinkle with the orange zest and juice. Put the coconut in a line next to the oats and sprinkle with the cinnamon. Continuing the striped pattern, add the almonds, sunflower seeds, pumpkin seeds, sesame seeds, and buckwheat. Transfer the sheet to the oven and bake for about 10 minutes or until the seeds are golden. Set aside to cool completely.

Transfer the contents of the baking sheet to a bowl and mix with the flaxseeds, amaranth, and dried fruit.

Serve with grated apple and/or blueberries, if using, and your choice of low-fat milk, soy milk, or plain yogurt.

The muesli will stay fresh for several weeks in an airtight container in the fridge (it should be stored cold to prevent the nuts and seeds from becoming rancid).

Add some walnuts or pecans to the mix, and if you're serving large numbers, layer the fruit, muesli, and yogurt with some torn mint on a platter.

With or without cooking the oats and nuts, you can soak the oats, nuts, and seeds in ½ cup low-fat milk and ½ cup orange juice (with no added sugar) overnight to make a delicious bircher-style muesli. To serve, simply add a little low-GI fruit and yogurt and, if you like, a combination of lecithin granules, wheat germ, and/or oat bran.

Grilled Peaches with Bacon, Cinnamon Ricotta and Pear Syrup

SERVES 2

Prep time: 10 minutes

Cooking time: 10 minutes

Olive oil spray

4 slices lean bacon, fat removed

2 ripe peaches, pits removed, each
sliced into 8 segments

¼ cup low-fat ricotta

Pinch of ground cinnamon

2 slices light rye or low-GI whole grain
bread

2 teaspoons pear or apple juice
concentrate

243 calories; 15 g protein; 22 g carb; 11 g
fat; 5 g saturated fat; 35 mg cholesterol;
5 g fiber; 682 mg sodium

This is especially good when fresh peaches and nectarines are in season, but it also works well with canned peaches in natural juice.

Heat a nonstick grill pan over medium heat and spray with oil. Add the bacon and cook for 2 to 3 minutes on each side or until lightly golden. After 1 to 2 minutes add the peach segments and cook each side until golden.

Meanwhile, gently mix together the ricotta and cinnamon.

Toast or grill the bread if you like and place a piece on each plate. Top with the bacon, ricotta, and peach segments, then drizzle with the pear juice concentrate and serve.

Peaches are a low-GI fruit, but for a lower-carb, savory option use two firm ripe tomatoes instead of the peaches, low-fat cottage cheese instead of ricotta, shredded basil instead of the cinnamon, and vincotto in place of the pear juice concentrate.

≡ Replace the berries with canned peaches or shredded apples when berries are out of season.

French Toast Stack with Cottage Cheese and Berries

While this is not strictly a low-carb breakfast, it is low GI, high in protein, and (with the berries) full of antioxidants and folate. It makes a great start to the day.

Gently whisk together the egg, orange zest, and vanilla. Use a small cookie cutter or drinking glass to make three small bread circles for each person, then briefly submerge the bread rounds in the egg mixture.

Heat a nonstick frying pan over medium-high heat and add the butter and oil. When sizzling, add the eggy bread and cook for 1 to 2 minutes on each side or until golden.

To serve, slide three bread rounds onto each plate, top with cottage cheese and berries, and drizzle with a little maple syrup. Sprinkle a little shredded mint over the top, if desired.

The maple syrup may be replaced with pear or apple juice concentrate or fig vincotto.

Kid Friendly Use low-fat cream cheese instead of the cottage cheese.

SERVES 2
Prep time: 10 minutes
Cooking time: 5 minutes

1 large egg
1 teaspoon grated orange zest
½ teaspoon vanilla extract
3 to 4 pieces low-GI whole grain bread (depending on the size of the bread and the cutter)
1 teaspoon butter
Olive oil spray
¼ cup low-fat cottage cheese
1 cup blueberries or mixed berries
1 tablespoon pure maple syrup
Shredded mint, optional

252 calories; 13 g protein; 38 g carb; 6 g fat; 1 g saturated fat; 112 mg cholesterol; 10 g fiber; 257 mg sodium

Breakfast Shakes

These high-protein, low-GI fruit shakes are a great breakfast solution when you don't have a lot of time in the morning, or you can enjoy them later in the day as a nutritious pick-me-up.

Experiment with different low-GI fruit and ingredients, such as wheat germ, lecithin granules, amaranth, and different seeds, or try soy milk or orange, pineapple, pear, or apple juice (with no added sugar) in varying quantities. Adding a couple of tablespoons of yogurt that contains acidophilus bifidus is a great way to include a probiotic in your daily diet. A few drops of rosewater or mint water add a subtle flavor, but don't overdo it—a little goes a long way!

All of these recipes make one shake. Simply place the ingredients in a blender, process until smooth, and serve in a tall glass.

▶ Crushed Pineapple, Orange and Ginger Shake

½ cup canned crushed pineapple (with no added sugar)
½ orange, peeled, seeds removed
1 to 2 teaspoons grated ginger (to taste)
3 tablespoons vanilla protein powder
⅓ to ½ cup low-fat milk or soy milk
Small handful of ice
1 tablespoon LSA (page 13)

264 calories; 18 g protein; 38 g carb; 6 g fat; 1 g saturated fat; 9 mg cholesterol; 4 g fiber; 173 mg sodium

▶ Pear, Apple and Soy Thick Shake

½ apple, skin on, roughly chopped
½ ripe pear (or use 5 slices canned pear in natural juice)
1 teaspoon pear or apple juice concentrate (or 3 tablespoons pear juice from the can)
3 tablespoons vanilla protein powder
1 tablespoon wheat germ
2 tablespoons passionfruit pulp
⅓ to ½ cup low-fat soy milk
Small handful of ice

256 calories; 17 g protein; 42 g carb; 4 g fat; 0 g saturated fat; 6 mg cholesterol; 10 g fiber; 139 mg sodium

▶ Peach, Strawberry and Vanilla Soy Smoothie

½ cup strawberries
½ cup canned peaches in natural juice
3 tablespoons vanilla protein powder
1 teaspoon vanilla extract
⅓ to ½ cup low-fat soy milk or milk
Small handful of ice
1 tablespoon LSA (page 13)
Pomegranate seeds, to garnish, optional

251 calories; 15 g protein; 34 g carb; 6 g fat; 0 g saturated fat; 6 mg cholesterol; 5 g fiber; 162 mg sodium

▶ Orange, Berry and Mint Shake

½ orange, peeled, seeds removed
½ cup fresh or frozen mixed berries
3 tablespoons vanilla protein powder
⅓ to ½ cup low-fat milk
Small handful of ice
2 tablespoons finely chopped mint, optional

177 calories; 15 g protein; 27 g carb; 2 g fat; 1 g saturated fat; 9 mg cholesterol; 4 g fiber; 162 mg sodium

≡ If you find the shakes are a little thick, add more milk or water.

≡ Replace the cherry tomatoes with six finely sliced sun-dried tomatoes, if preferred.

Open Omelette with Cherry Tomatoes, Basil and Olives

I love the intensity of flavors the basil and olives bring to this omelette. It's particularly delicious served with crispbread.

Gently whisk together the egg, egg whites, cottage cheese, and basil and season with salt and pepper.

Heat a small nonstick frying pan over medium heat. When hot, lightly spray with oil, then pour in the egg mixture. Cook for 2 to 3 minutes, then dot the olives, tomatoes, and cheese over the omelette. Reduce the heat to low, then place a lid over the pan and cook for another 3 to 4 minutes or until the omelette is cooked through. Alternatively, finish cooking under the broiler for a golden finish.

To serve, arrange some of the arugula on two plates. Cut the omelette in half and slide onto the leaves. Scatter the remaining arugula over the top and serve.

Cut ¼ firm avocado into cubes and combine with a tablespoon each of finely chopped red onion and crumbled goat cheese or low-fat tzatziki. Dollop over the arugula.

If you don't have any fresh basil, stir 2 teaspoons of dried basil or arugula pesto into the egg mixture instead.

SERVES 2
Prep time: 5 minutes
Cooking time: 10 minutes

3 large eggs
2 large egg whites
3 tablespoons low-fat cottage cheese
½ cup chopped basil
Flaky sea salt and freshly ground black pepper to taste
Olive oil spray
8 marinated kalamata olives, pitted and squashed
8 cherry tomatoes, roughly chopped
2 tablespoons soft goat cheese or feta marinated in olive oil
2 cups arugula

253 calories; 19 g protein; 7 g carb; 14 g fat; 6 g saturated fat; 326 mg cholesterol; 1 g fiber; 719 mg sodium

High Protein, Low GI, Bold Flavor

< Open Omelette with Ricotta and Sauteed Mushrooms

This features regularly on our breakfast menu—the thyme and ricotta make it tasty and light.

Serves 2 | Prep time: 10 minutes | Cooking time: 10 minutes

1 teaspoon butter
Olive oil spray
4 ounces white mushrooms, finely sliced (about 4 medium mushrooms)
1 tablespoon finely chopped thyme, plus extra leaves to garnish
3 large eggs
2 large egg whites
2 tablespoons low-fat ricotta
Flaky sea salt and freshly ground black pepper to taste
1 cup baby spinach
2 tablespoons shredded Jarlsberg or Parmesan

Heat a medium nonstick frying pan over medium heat, add the butter, and spray with oil. Add the mushrooms and thyme and cook for 2 to 3 minutes, then remove and place in a bowl. Wipe out the pan.

Gently whisk together the eggs, egg whites, ricotta, and 2 teaspoons water and season with salt and pepper. Return the pan to low heat and add a little more oil. Pour in the egg mixture and cook for 2 to 3 minutes, then arrange the mushroom mixture and spinach evenly over the omelette. Sprinkle with cheese, then place a lid over the pan and cook for another 3 to 4 minutes. Turn off the heat and leave with the lid on for a minute or two until the omelette is cooked through. Alternatively, finish cooking under the broiler for a golden finish.

Cut the omelette in half, then slide onto two plates and serve.

206 calories; 19 g protein; 5 g carb; 12 g fat; 4 g saturated fat; 335 mg cholesterol; 1 g fiber; 489 mg sodium

Open Omelette with Asparagus, Shaved Turkey and Gruyère

Use low-fat cheddar or a little goat cheese instead of Gruyère, if preferred, or replace the chives with chopped basil, cilantro, dill, or flat-leaf parsley.

Serves 2 | Prep time: 10 minutes | Cooking time: 5 minutes

8 thick asparagus spears (or use 12 to 14 thinner spears or 2 bunches baby asparagus)
3 large eggs
2 large egg whites
½ cup finely chopped chives
Flaky sea salt and freshly ground black pepper to taste
Olive oil spray
3 ounces thinly sliced cooked turkey breast
¼ cup grated Gruyère

Snap the asparagus spears where they break naturally (this removes the woody ends) and lightly steam or microwave until just tender. Leave them whole or cut them into bite-sized pieces on the diagonal.

Gently whisk together the eggs, egg whites, 1 tablespoon water, and most of the chives (reserve 1 tablespoon for garnish). Season with salt and pepper.

Heat a medium nonstick frying pan over medium heat. Lightly spray with oil, then pour in the egg mixture and cook for 2 to 3 minutes. Scatter the turkey over the egg, followed by the asparagus, then sprinkle with the cheese. Place a lid over the pan and cook for another 3 to 4 minutes or until the omelette is cooked through. If the base appears to be cooking too quickly, turn off the heat and leave with the lid on for a minute or two until the omelette is cooked through. Alternatively, finish cooking under the broiler for a golden finish.

Cut the omelette in half, then slide onto two plates. Sprinkle with the reserved chives and serve.

256 calories; 29 g protein; 7 g carb; 13 g fat; 5 g saturated fat; 352 mg cholesterol; 2 g fiber; 503 mg sodium

Smoked Salmon, Dill and Caper Frittata

SERVES 2
Prep time: 10 minutes
Cooking time: 5 minutes

4 large eggs
2 large egg whites
½ cup light evaporated milk
¼ cup finely chopped dill
Flaky sea salt and freshly ground
    black pepper to taste
Olive oil spray
4 ounces smoked salmon, torn into
    large pieces
1 tablespoon capers
2 vine-ripened tomatoes, finely
    chopped
2 tablespoons low-fat tzatziki (page 15)

---

372 calories; 35 g protein; 16 g carb; 19 g
fat; 7 g saturated fat; 470 mg cholesterol;
1 g fiber; 1523 mg sodium

I must admit I don't usually cook smoked salmon, but it works wonderfully here with the bite of capers and fresh tzatziki. Canned salmon also works well; either form provides plenty of protein.

Preheat the broiler to medium.

Vigorously whisk together the eggs, egg whites, milk, and half the dill and season with salt and pepper.

Heat a medium nonstick frying pan over medium heat and lightly spray with oil. Add the egg mixture, then reduce the heat to medium–low and cook for 2 to 3 minutes. Sprinkle the smoked salmon over the egg mixture, then place under the broiler for 2 to 3 minutes or until golden and cooked through.

Meanwhile, combine the capers, tomatoes, and remaining dill.

Slide the frittata onto a serving plate, scatter the tomato mixture over the top, and finish with a few dollops of tzatziki.

Take care not to have the heat too high or it will burn the bottom. If the bottom is cooking too quickly, take the pan off the heat and finish cooking under the broiler. If you are not sure whether your pan has an ovenproof handle, simply wrap it in foil.

For added flavor, first slice the white part of a leek and saute in a little oil over medium heat. When the leek is soft and golden, pour the egg mixture over the top and continue with the recipe.

High Protein, Low GI, Bold Flavor

Dill and Ricotta Pancakes with Smoked Salmon and Spinach

These pancakes are delicious, protein-rich, and healthy—the smoked salmon and spinach are both high in antioxidants and rich in vitamins E and C, and the omega-3 in the fish will help to fight heart disease. If you prefer, make one large pancake and slice it in half.

Gently whisk together the eggs, ricotta, and half the dill to form a batter.

In a separate bowl, combine the cottage cheese, lemon juice, and remaining dill. Season with salt and pepper.

Heat a small nonstick frying pan over medium heat and lightly spray with oil. Pour in half the batter to make three small pancakes and cook for 1 to 1½ minutes on each side. Remove and keep warm while you cook the remaining pancakes.

To serve, place three pancakes on each plate. Spread the cottage cheese mixture over the pancakes, then place a few spinach leaves on top. Stack the smoked salmon on the spinach and season with salt and pepper. Drizzle with a little vincotto or balsamic vinegar, if desired.

Play around with the ingredients to suit your own tastes. Other herbs may be used in place of the dill—try basil, chives, or 2 teaspoons basil pesto. Replace the cottage cheese with low-fat sour cream, cream cheese, or tzatziki. You might also like to add 2 tablespoons corn kernels to the pancake batter.

These are delicious with a few slices of avocado and a drizzle of lemon olive oil.

SERVES 2
Prep time: 10 minutes
Cooking time: 5 minutes

2 large eggs
¼ cup plus 2 tablespoons low-fat ricotta
2 tablespoons finely chopped dill
2 tablespoons low-fat cottage cheese, drained of any excess liquid
Good squeeze of lemon juice
Flaky sea salt and freshly ground black pepper to taste
Olive oil spray
1½ cups baby spinach
4 ounces smoked salmon
Vincotto or aged balsamic vinegar, optional

220 calories; 28 g protein; 5 g carb; 11 g fat; 4 g saturated fat; 245 mg cholesterol; 1 g fiber; 1149 mg sodium

Sardines in Tomato Sauce

For a long time sardines were not high on my list of favorite foods, but I have been converted. They are so delicious in this simple combination, and wonderfully good for you.

Serves 2 | Prep time: 10 minutes | Cooking time: 5 minutes

½ cup homemade tomato sauce (page 130) or ready-made
   tomato pasta sauce or passata
One 4-ounce can sardines in spring water, drained
2 slices light rye or low-GI whole grain bread, toasted
½ avocado, sliced
1 tablespoon grated lemon zest
Squeeze of lemon juice
Freshly ground black pepper to taste

Heat the tomato sauce in a small saucepan over low heat. Add the sardines and gently cook for 2 to 3 minutes or until warmed through.

To serve, place a piece of toast on each plate and spoon the sardines and sauce over the top. Layer the avocado over the sardines and sprinkle with lemon zest and a squeeze of lemon juice. Season with the pepper.

369 calories; 17 g protein; 36 g carb; 21 g fat; 1 g saturated fat; 0 mg cholesterol; 6 g fiber; 481 mg sodium

Sardines are an excellent source of protein, calcium, vitamins A, B_2, B_{12}, and niacin, and omega-3 oil and should be included in your weekly diet.

Smoked Salmon and Avocado with Vincotto >

Reduce the carbs in this nutritious breakfast by using low-carb crispbread, or forget the bread altogether and serve the salmon on lean bacon, with lettuce as a base.

Serves 2 | Prep time: 10 minutes | Cooking time: 1 minute

2 slices light rye or low-GI whole grain bread
¼ cup low-fat cottage cheese
4 ounces smoked salmon
1 avocado, sliced
1 tablespoon finely chopped chives
1 tablespoon finely chopped red onion, optional
Capers, optional
1 teaspoon vincotto
Lemon wedges, to serve, optional

Toast or grill the bread if you like and spread with cottage cheese. Place the salmon and avocado on top and sprinkle with the chives, onion, and capers, if using. Finish with a drizzle of vincotto and serve with lemon wedges, if desired.

266 calories; 19 g protein; 21 g carb; 13 g fat; 3 g saturated fat; 25 mg cholesterol; 4 g fiber; 940 mg sodium

This is also delicious with smoked ocean trout, canned tuna, or shaved turkey instead of salmon. For a lower-fat option, use tomato instead of avocado.

If vincotto is unavailable, use apple balsamic or reduced balsamic vinegar.

☰ To add a bit of extra punch, mix a little grated horseradish with the cottage cheese.

Eggplant, Spinach and Ricotta Lasagna

SERVES 8
Prep time: 30 minutes
Cooking time: 1 hour 35 minutes

2 large eggplants, cut into ½-inch-
thick rounds
Flaky sea salt and freshly ground
black pepper to taste
1½ pounds spinach
3 cups tomato passata or tomato
sauce
2 tablespoons tomato paste
4 garlic cloves, finely chopped
1 cup chicken stock
1½ cups chopped flat-leaf parsley
and/or basil
1 large egg
1 cup low-fat ricotta
1 cup low-fat cottage cheese
Olive oil spray
½ cup grated Parmesan

192 calories; 18 g protein; 23 g carb; 5 g fat;
2 g saturated fat; 39 mg cholesterol; 8 g
fiber; 491 mg sodium

This takes a little time to prepare, but you can do it all in advance and reheat it when you're ready to eat. Served with a green salad, it makes the perfect light lunch for a crowd.

Preheat the oven to 350°F.

Sprinkle the eggplant slices with salt and set aside for 15 minutes.

Meanwhile, wash and coarsely chop the spinach, then place in a colander and shake well (you still want a little water clinging to the leaves). Place in a large sauce-pan over medium heat and cook for 3 to 4 minutes or until wilted, stirring after a minute or two to stop the spinach from sticking to the pan and burning. Return to the colander and squeeze out as much liquid as you can.

Pour the tomato passata into the pan and heat over medium-high heat. Add the tomato paste, garlic, stock, and 1 cup of the parsley and simmer for 15 to 20 minutes.

Meanwhile, whisk together the egg, ricotta, and cottage cheese and season with salt and pepper. Stir in the spinach.

Rinse the eggplant slices, then pat dry with paper towels. Heat two large nonstick frying pans over medium-high heat and spray with oil. Add the eggplant slices and cook for 3 to 4 minutes. Turn the slices, spraying the pan with a little more oil, and cook for another 3 to 4 minutes. Remove and drain on paper towels. (You can do this in one frying pan if you like, I suggest two pans only to reduce the cooking time, as there are quite a few slices to fry.)

Spray a 9 × 13-inch nonstick lasagna or baking dish with oil, then layer with the tomato sauce, eggplant slices, and cheese mixture. Repeat until all the ingredients have been used, finishing with a layer of tomato sauce, and sprinkle with the remaining herbs. Cover with foil and bake for 45 minutes. Remove the foil and sprinkle with the Parmesan, then return the lasagna to the oven for another 15 to 20 minutes or until cooked through. Cover with foil again if it starts to brown too much on top.

If you can find it, try fresh, firm ricotta, available in some delis, rather than the spreadable version in the dairy section of supermarkets.

≡ For a higher-carb option (but still low GI), add a couple of layers of lasagna sheets.

Leek and Zucchini Crustless Pie

Like the lasagna on the previous page, this light, flavorful dish is perfect for sharing with friends for lunch. My son loves it sliced and toasted in a wrap with a little grated cheddar—another great snack idea, which can be adopted with any type of omelette or frittata.

Preheat the oven to 350°F.

Place the grated zucchini in a colander and squeeze out as much liquid as possible.

Heat the oil in a large frying pan over medium-high heat and cook the leek and zucchini for 4 minutes or until the zucchini has softened, stirring constantly. Return the mixture to the colander and remove any excess liquid by pressing with paper towels.

Add the bacon to the pan and cook for 1 to 2 minutes.

Meanwhile, vigorously whisk together the eggs, dill, salt and pepper, and half the Parmesan. Add the bacon, leek, and zucchini to the egg mixture and stir well.

Spray a 9-inch pie pan with oil. Pour in the bacon and vegetable mixture and bake for 15 minutes. Sprinkle with the remaining Parmesan and bake for another 20 to 25 minutes or until golden and cooked through. Serve with a green salad.

SERVES 4
Prep time: 15 minutes
Cooking time: 45 minutes

3 to 4 zucchini, grated
1 tablespoon olive oil
1 leek, white part only, finely sliced
6 slices lean bacon, fat removed, cut into ½-inch squares
6 large eggs
½ cup finely chopped dill
Flaky sea salt and freshly ground black pepper to taste
½ cup grated Parmesan
Olive oil spray

Green salad

323 calories; 23 g protein; 9 g carb; 22 g fat; 8 g saturated fat; 351 mg cholesterol; 2 g fiber; 880 mg sodium

You can further reduce the fat content by replacing the 6 whole eggs with 4 eggs, 2 egg whites, and ½ cup light evaporated milk. Also, if you line the pan with parchment paper you won't need to spray it with oil.

Main-Meal Soups

A bowl of homemade soup made with meat or chicken is often substantial enough to serve as a complete, nutritious meal. I also love to use lentils and beans, as they provide flavor, texture, and extra protein. Don't feel you have to follow the recipes exactly—use whatever ingredients you like. My only advice would be to use the best-quality stock you can lay your hands on.

Chicken and Corn Broth with Chicken Dumplings

This is a great meal for feeding kids en masse. Add half a cup of basmati rice for some extra low GI carbs.

SERVES 4
Prep time: 20 minutes
Cooking time: 15 minutes

8 cups chicken stock
8 large scallions, finely sliced through
    to the end
1 cup corn kernels, sliced off the cob
    in strips
1 large red chile, seeded and finely
    sliced, optional

CHICKEN DUMPLINGS
12 ounces lean ground chicken (or try
    ground turkey or veal)
2 tablespoons finely chopped scallions
¼ cup finely chopped water chestnuts,
    optional
½ cup finely chopped flat-leaf parsley
3 tablespoons grated Parmesan
¼ cup ground almonds
2 tablespoons tomato paste
2 tablespoons pear or apple juice
    concentrate
Pinch of table salt

---

250 calories; 27 g protein; 18 g carb; 8 g fat;
1 g saturated fat; 62 mg cholesterol; 4 g
fiber; 370 mg sodium

To make the chicken dumplings, combine all the ingredients in a bowl and mix well. With wet hands, roll the mixture into dumplings about the size of walnuts.

Pour the stock into a large heavy-bottomed saucepan and add most of the scallions (reserve a little for garnish). Bring to a boil, then reduce the heat so the broth is just simmering. Gently add the dumplings and cook for about 10 minutes, stirring occasionally, until cooked through. Add the corn and cook for another minute.

Ladle the soup and dumplings into deep bowls and sprinkle with the reserved scallions and red chile, if using. Serve with a crusty low-GI roll or some warm bread, if desired.

Gently whisk 2 lightly beaten eggs through the soup when the dumplings are ready and cook for another 1 to 2 minutes.

Kid Friendly Forget the water chestnuts in the dumplings, and replace with a handful of finely chopped basil. Cook them in homemade tomato sauce (page 130) and serve over some durum-wheat rigatoni or farfalle with a sprinkling of grated mozzarella or Parmesan. A totally new dish—lean protein, vegetables, fiber, and low-GI carbs!

Try adding some chopped cilantro to the dumplings or for garnish.

Veal Shank, Cauliflower and Barley Soup

This satisfying slow-cooked meal can be made with 6 lamb shanks instead of the veal, if preferred. If you can, make it the day before you need it to give the flavors time to develop.

Serves 6 | Prep time: 15 minutes | Cooking time: 2 hours

12 small foreleg veal shanks (4 to 5 ounces each)
Flaky sea salt and freshly ground black pepper to taste
1 tablespoon olive oil
10 cups beef or chicken stock or a combination of both
2 garlic cloves, sliced
1 onion, finely chopped
4 celery stalks, finely chopped
2 carrots, sliced on the diagonal into 1-inch pieces
½ cup pearl barley, rinsed and drained
6 sprigs thyme, plus 2 extra sprigs to garnish
6 sprigs rosemary
1 pound cauliflower, broken into large florets

Season the veal shanks with salt and pepper. Heat the oil in a large heavy-bottomed saucepan over medium heat, add the shanks, and cook for 2 minutes on each side or until golden, adding a little stock if the meat starts to stick. Remove and drain on paper towels.

Reduce the heat to medium–low. Add the garlic, onion, celery, and carrots and cook for 3 to 4 minutes, adding a little more stock if the vegetables start to stick. Stir in the pearl barley, thyme, rosemary, and remaining stock and return the veal to the pan. Bring to a boil, then reduce the heat and simmer gently, partially covered, for 45 minutes. Add the cauliflower and simmer, covered, for another 45 to 60 minutes. Season with salt and pepper.

To serve, divide the veal shanks among six bowls and ladle the soup over the top.

473 calories; 66 g protein; 22 g carb; 13 g fat; 3 g saturated fat; 212 mg cholesterol; 6 g fiber; 560 mg sodium

For a last-minute flavor burst, roughly chop 1 cup of flat-leaf parsley and finely chop 4 cloves of garlic and add to the soup 15 minutes prior to serving.

Chicken and Spinach Soup >

A quick and easy soup that's sure to please even the fussiest palate. If you like, add flat egg noodles or quinoa for some additional low-GI carbs.

Serves 4 to 6 | Prep time: 15 minutes | Cooking time: 10 minutes

6 cups chicken stock
6 cups baby spinach
4 garlic cloves, finely chopped
¼ cup plus 2 tablespoons grated Parmesan
1 cup roughly chopped flat-leaf parsley
4 boneless, skinless chicken thighs, fat removed, cut into ½-inch slices
2 large eggs, very lightly beaten
Freshly ground black pepper to taste

Heat the stock in a large heavy-bottomed saucepan and bring to a boil. Add the spinach and simmer for 3 to 4 minutes. Stir in the garlic, 2 tablespoons of the Parmesan, parsley, and chicken pieces and cook, stirring, for 1 to 2 minutes. Vigorously whisk in the eggs and cook for another 3 to 4 minutes or until the chicken is cooked through.

Ladle the soup into bowls, garnish with the remaining Parmesan and pepper, and serve.

219 calories; 23 g protein; 11 g carb; 10 g fat; 3 g saturated fat; 177 mg cholesterol; 3 g fiber; 470 mg sodium

To make this a vegetarian soup, replace the chicken with 14 ounces firm tofu (cut into small cubes) and use vegetable stock instead of chicken stock.

☰ Pork fillets also work well in this recipe.

High Protein, Low GI, Bold Flavor

Lamb Shank, Mushroom and Puy Lentil Soup

Like many slow-cooked dishes, most of the work for this hearty soup is done in the first 30 minutes, and then you can sit back and relax while it bubbles away. It is delicious served with a sprinkling of freshly grated Parmesan.

Season the lamb with salt and pepper. Heat the oil in a large heavy-bottomed saucepan over medium heat and cook the lamb pieces for 2 to 3 minutes on each side until golden. Remove and drain on paper towels.

Add the celery, carrot, onion, lentils, and oregano to the pan and cook for about 3 to 4 minutes. Arrange the lamb shanks horizontally over the vegetables and add the stock and mushrooms. Bring the mixture to a boil, then reduce the heat and simmer, partially covered, for 1 to 1½ hours or until the meat is tender. About 10 minutes before serving, stir in the garlic and most of the parsley (reserve a little for garnish).

Divide the shanks among six bowls and ladle the soup over the top. Sprinkle with lemon zest and the remaining parsley and serve.

> You could also use trimmed lamb chops, if preferred, or even veal shanks.
>
> If you can't find fresh shiitake mushrooms, soak a cup of dried shiitakes in warm water for 30 minutes. Drain well and use these instead.

SERVES 6
Prep time: 15 minutes
Cooking time: 1 hour 40 minutes

Six 7-ounce lamb shanks, trimmed (see box)
Flaky sea salt and freshly ground black pepper to taste
1 tablespoon olive oil
2 celery stalks, finely chopped
1 carrot, finely chopped
1 onion, finely chopped
½ cup puy-style lentils, rinsed and drained
1 tablespoon dried oregano
7 cups chicken or beef stock
4 ounces shiitake or cremini mushrooms, stemmed and sliced
2 garlic cloves, finely chopped
½ cup roughly chopped flat-leaf parsley
Grated lemon zest

---

521 calories; 44 g protein; 15 g carb; 30 g fat; 12 g saturated fat; 149 mg cholesterol; 7 g fiber; 367 mg sodium

Pork, Chinese Cabbage and Mushroom Soup

The Asian flavors in this soup are subtle and beautifully balanced, but much depends on the quality of the chicken stock. If you don't have time to make your own, buy the best ready-made version you can afford.

Serves 4 to 6 | Prep time: 20 minutes | Cooking time: 15 minutes

8 cups chicken stock
8 large scallions, finely sliced
3 tablespoons grated ginger
4 ounces fresh shiitake mushrooms, finely sliced
7 ounces white mushrooms, finely sliced
¼ head Chinese cabbage, finely sliced
1 pound pork tenderloin, cut into ½-inch strips (or use boneless, skinless chicken thighs)
1 large egg, very lightly beaten

Combine the stock, scallions, ginger, and mushrooms in a large heavy-bottomed saucepan and bring to a boil. Add the cabbage, then reduce the heat and simmer for 3 to 4 minutes. Add the pork and cook for 1 to 2 minutes, then pour in the egg, stirring to make long strands. Simmer for another 3 to 4 minutes until the pork is cooked through.

Ladle the soup into bowls and serve.

252 calories; 31 g protein; 9 g carb; 10 g fat; 3 g saturated fat; 138 mg cholesterol; 2 g fiber; 304 mg sodium

Kid Friendly If your kids aren't keen on mushrooms, replace them with fresh corn. Using a sharp knife, simply cut the kernels off an ear of corn to make strips. Drained canned corn is fine if you don't have fresh.

Fast Tomato Soup with Crispy Pancetta >

Even your kids will agree, this is a vast improvement over canned tomato soup—without the added sugar! This is quite a light soup, and you may also like to have it as an appetizer (which would serve 6 to 8).

Serves 4 | Prep time: 10 minutes | Cooking time: 35 minutes

1 tablespoon olive oil
2 onions, coarsely chopped
Three 14.5-ounce cans diced tomatoes (with no added sugar)
½ cup tomato paste
2 cups chicken stock
1½ tablespoons balsamic vinegar, optional
1 cup fresh orange juice
4 garlic cloves, roughly chopped
Olive oil spray
8 slices pancetta
2 tablespoons low-fat ricotta or low-fat sour cream, optional
Chopped chives, to garnish
Flaky sea salt and freshly ground black pepper to taste

Heat the oil in a large heavy-bottomed saucepan over medium–low heat and cook the onions for 2 to 3 minutes or until softened. Add the tomatoes, tomato paste, stock, balsamic vinegar, orange juice, and garlic. Bring to a boil, then reduce the heat and simmer, covered, for 30 minutes. Remove from the heat and allow to cool slightly, then puree with an immersion blender or in a blender, retaining some texture.

Meanwhile, heat a nonstick frying pan over medium-high heat and spray with oil. Add the pancetta and cook for 1 minute on each side or until crisp. Break into long spears.

Ladle the soup into bowls and arrange the pancetta spears over the soup. Dollop with ricotta or sour cream, if using, sprinkle with chives, and season with salt and pepper.

304 calories; 13 g protein; 29 g carb; 14 g fat; 4 g saturated fat; 33 mg cholesterol; 5 g fiber; 865 mg sodium

Convert this into a vegetarian dish by using vegetable stock and leaving out the pancetta. Vegetarian or not, the soup is delicious served with ½ cup quinoa added with the stock and grated Parmesan. A dollop of pesto is always great with tomato dishes of any kind.

☰ Fresh is best, so if you have time, use 12 to 14 roughly chopped large tomatoes rather than the canned variety.

Osso Bucco and Sticky Onion Soup

SERVES 6 TO 8
Prep time: 20 minutes
Cooking time: 2 hours

1¾ pounds beef shanks
Flaky sea salt and freshly ground
    black pepper to taste
Olive oil spray
1½ tablespoons butter
1 tablespoon olive oil
8 large red onions, finely sliced
1 cup white or red wine
4 cups beef stock
4 cups chicken stock
1 tablespoon Dijon mustard
1 tablespoon Vegemite, optional (but
    delicious)
8 garlic cloves, finely chopped
1 cup finely chopped flat-leaf parsley,
    plus extra leaves to garnish
Grated Gruyère, pecorino, or
    Parmesan, optional

424 calories; 34 g protein; 20 g carb; 20 g fat; 5 g saturated fat; 62 mg cholesterol; 4 g fiber; 397 mg sodium

Don't be horrified by the amount of onions in this recipe—the slow cooking mellows their flavor and gives the soup a lovely stickiness. Slice the onions in a food processor to save time and avoid tears in your soup.

Lightly season the beef shanks with salt and pepper. Heat a very large heavy-bottomed saucepan over medium heat. Lightly spray with oil, then add the beef shanks and cook for 2 minutes on each side. Remove and drain on paper towels.

Add the butter and oil to the pan and, when sizzling, add the onions and stir well. Increase the heat and cook for about 30 minutes or until lightly golden and sticky, stirring frequently to keep the onions from sticking to the pan (add a little water or stock if they start to stick). Pour in the wine and bring to a boil, then add the stock, mustard, Vegemite, if using, and half the garlic and bring back to a boil. Return the beef shanks to the pan, then reduce the heat and simmer, partially covered, for 1 to 1½ hours. About 5 minutes before serving, stir in the parsley and remaining garlic.

Divide the osso bucco among serving bowls and ladle the soup over the top. Garnish with parsley and sprinkle with a little grated cheese, if desired.

Osso bucco literally means "bone with a hole" and refers to the part of a veal, lamb, or beef shank that has a tasty marrow filling. I usually use beef shanks for this recipe, but lamb shanks or lamb chops (trimmed of fat) would make a delicious variation.

Add a can of drained and rinsed cannellini beans to boost the levels of protein, fiber, and low-GI carbs.

High Protein, Low GI, Bold Flavor

Creamy Swiss Chard and Leek Soup

This unusual soup has always been a surprise hit with my children.

Serves 4 | Prep time: 15 minutes | Cooking time: 35 minutes

1 tablespoon olive oil
1 onion, roughly chopped
2 large leeks, white part only, roughly chopped
2 garlic cloves, roughly chopped
1 teaspoon curry powder
1 large bunch Swiss chard (about 1½ pounds), stalks removed, leaves roughly chopped
4 cups chicken stock
½ cup low-fat milk or light evaporated milk
Flaky sea salt and freshly ground black pepper to taste
1 tablespoon low-fat sour cream or low-fat cream cheese, optional
1 tablespoon fried shallots (page 14), optional

Heat the oil in a large heavy-bottomed saucepan over medium heat, add the onion, leeks, garlic, and curry powder, and cook, stirring, for 3 to 4 minutes. Add the Swiss chard and cook for another 10 minutes.

Pour in the stock and bring to a boil, then reduce the heat and simmer, covered, for 20 minutes. Allow to cool slightly, then puree with an immersion blender or in a blender. Stir in the milk and gently reheat. Season with salt and pepper.

To serve, ladle the soup into bowls, garnish with a little sour cream or cream cheese if desired, and sprinkle a few fried shallots over the top, if using.

126 calories; 5 g protein; 16 g carb; 5 g fat; 0 g saturated fat; 6 mg cholesterol; 3 g fiber; 504 mg sodium

Add 1 cup frozen peas and 1 to 2 tablespoons chopped mint with the Swiss chard for extra fiber, vitamins, and minerals. The mint blends beautifully with the curry flavor. A few whole peas look great with the sour cream as a garnish.

Moroccan Cabbage, Cannellini Bean and Cilantro Soup

The beans push this soup to the higher end of the carb scale, but it is low GI, high in fiber, nutritiously dense, and absolutely delicious!

Serves 4 | Prep time: 15 minutes | Cooking time: 35 minutes

1 tablespoon olive oil
6 scallions, sliced
1 carrot, roughly chopped
¼ head savoy cabbage, roughly sliced
1 teaspoon ground cumin
1 tablespoon grated ginger or 1 teaspoon ground ginger
One 15-ounce can cannellini beans, rinsed and drained
2 cups beef stock
½ cup cilantro leaves
Flaky sea salt and freshly ground black pepper to taste

Heat the oil in a large heavy-bottomed saucepan over medium heat and cook the scallions, carrot, and cabbage for 4 to 5 minutes, stirring frequently. Add the cumin, ginger, and half the beans and cook for another minute. Pour in the stock and 1 cup water and increase the heat. Bring to a boil, then reduce the heat and simmer, covered, for 30 minutes. Add half the cilantro, then allow to cool slightly. Puree with an immersion blender or in a blender.

Return the soup to the pan and stir in the remaining beans and most of the remaining cilantro (reserve a few leaves for garnish). Season with salt and pepper. Ladle the soup into bowls and top with the reserved cilantro.

157 calories; 9 g protein; 22 g carb; 4 g fat; 0 g saturated fat; 0 mg cholesterol; 7 g fiber; 458 mg sodium

Drizzle with a little lemon olive oil, an extra pinch of cumin, or freshly grated Parmesan just before serving.

Sweet Potato, Pumpkin and Ginger Soup with Coconut Milk

SERVES 4 TO 6
Prep time: 20 minutes
Cooking time: 40 minutes

1 tablespoon olive oil
1 onion, roughly chopped
12 ounces pumpkin, diced
12 ounces sweet potato, diced
½ cup red or puy-style lentils, rinsed
    and drained
4 garlic cloves, finely chopped
3 tablespoons grated ginger (or less,
    to taste)
4 cups chicken stock
½ cup roughly chopped cilantro, plus
    extra leaves to garnish
½ cup light coconut milk

253 calories; 10 g protein; 39 g carb; 7 g fat; 2 g saturated fat; 5 mg cholesterol; 10 g fiber; 115 mg sodium

The pumpkin is high GI, but by mixing it with low-GI sweet potato and lentils and the fat of the coconut milk, the soup is still low GI. I adore ginger and use it in generous quantities, but you may want to add less to suit your family's tastes.

Heat the oil in a large heavy-bottomed saucepan over medium-high heat and cook the onion for 2 to 3 minutes or until transparent. Add the pumpkin, sweet potato, and lentils and cook for another 3 to 4 minutes, stirring frequently. Add the garlic and ginger and mix well, then pour in the stock. Bring to a boil, then reduce the heat and simmer, covered, for 20 minutes. Add the cilantro and cook for another 10 minutes or until the vegetables and lentils are tender. Stir in the coconut milk.

Ladle the soup into deep bowls and garnish with extra cilantro leaves.

If you prefer a thick, smooth consistency, puree the soup with an immersion blender or in a blender. Garnish with a little extra coconut milk and some fried shallots (page 14).

To make this a vegetarian soup, simply replace the chicken stock with your favorite vegetable stock.

≡ Play around with garnishes—try a drizzle of lemon olive oil or truffle oil and a sprinkling of ground cumin.

Cauliflower and Celeriac Soup

This wonderfully comforting soup has a delicious, unusual flavor that will keep your fellow diners guessing.

Heat the oil in a large heavy-bottomed saucepan over medium-high heat and cook the onion for 2 to 3 minutes. Add the celeriac, cauliflower, and beans and cook for another 3 to 4 minutes, stirring frequently. Pour in the stock. Increase the heat and bring to a boil, then reduce the heat and simmer, covered, for 15 to 20 minutes or until the vegetables are cooked through. Allow to cool slightly, then puree with an immersion blender or in a blender. Season with salt and pepper.

Ladle the soup into bowls and finish with a drizzle of extra virgin olive oil.

If you don't like celeriac or it is out of season, simply increase the quantity of cauliflower. Or you could leave out the cauliflower altogether and use one large fennel bulb instead.

Another lovely garnish for this soup is some shaved Parmesan and a good grinding of black pepper.

SERVES 4 TO 6
Prep time: 15 minutes
Cooking time: 30 minutes

1 tablespoon olive oil
1 onion, roughly chopped
8 ounces celeriac, roughly chopped
1 pound cauliflower, roughly chopped
One 15-ounce can cannellini beans, rinsed and drained
4 cups chicken stock
Flaky sea salt and freshly ground black pepper to taste
Extra virgin olive oil

226 calories; 10 g protein; 36 g carb; 6 g fat; 0 g saturated fat; 5 mg cholesterol; 10 g fiber; 591 mg sodium

Main-Meal Salads

This is a great way to eat when you are following a "green-and-protein" diet because anything goes! If you keep your kitchen well stocked with fresh salad leaves, vegetables, herbs, soft cheeses, capers, olives, and a few cans of tuna, salmon, or beans, you can always come up with something exciting and satisfying. Toasted seeds or nuts scattered over the top add crunch and flavor.

Chinese Salmon, Radish and Cucumber Salad

SERVES 4

Prep time: 30 minutes
Cooking time: 20 minutes

Two 7-ounce salmon fillets
2 tablespoons low-sodium tamari or
    soy sauce
2 teaspoons pure maple syrup
4 radishes, shredded or grated
½ head Chinese cabbage, finely
    shredded
½ English cucumber, peeled, seeded,
    finely shredded or thinly sliced
1 large carrot, peeled into long strips
    or shredded
4 ounces snow peas, sliced lengthwise
1½ cups cilantro leaves
1 small red chile, seeded and finely
    chopped
½ cup Vietnamese mint leaves

SOY AND GINGER DRESSING
1 tablespoon low-sodium tamari or soy
    sauce
1 teaspoon pure maple syrup or honey
1 tablespoon lemon juice
1 tablespoon rice wine vinegar
2 teaspoons sesame oil
1 teaspoon grated ginger

239 calories; 26 g protein; 15 g carb; 9 g
fat; 1 g saturated fat; 44 mg cholesterol;
3 g fiber; 535 mg sodium

Vietnamese mint is quite hot and is usually only available at Asian food stores or markets. If you can't find it or would prefer your salad to have a milder flavor, use regular mint instead.

Preheat the oven to 350°F.

Place the salmon fillets in a baking dish. Combine the tamari and maple syrup and drizzle over the salmon. Cover with parchment paper and bake for 15 minutes. Remove and leave to cool, then gently flake or slice the flesh.

Meanwhile, to make the dressing, place all the ingredients in a glass jar with a lid and shake well.

Combine the flaked salmon, the remaining salad ingredients, and the dressing in a large bowl and toss well. Pile the salad onto plates and serve.

For a quick alternative, simply cook the salmon in a grill pan over medium-high heat for 2 minutes on each side. Or use roast salmon portions, which are available at most supermarkets. They are quite rich so you will not need as much.

Shredded chicken would make a nice change from the salmon in this salad. Poach 2 chicken breasts in just-simmering stock for 10 minutes, then remove the pan from the heat and let the chicken stand for another 10 minutes. Shred the chicken and proceed with the recipe.

Using a mandoline or a food processor to shred the salad ingredients will cut the prep time in half.

≡ Garnish with toasted sesame seeds or almonds, or try a handful of fried shallots.

Roast Salmon with Orange, Fennel and Cannellini Beans

Black sesame seeds are available from Asian food stores and most good supermarkets. If you can't find them, use poppy seeds or toasted white sesame seeds instead.

Serves 2 | Prep time: 15 minutes

2 oranges
½ large fennel bulb, finely sliced
½ salad onion, finely sliced
4 cups baby spinach
Two 3-ounce roast salmon portions, gently flaked
½ cup canned cannellini beans or chickpeas, rinsed and drained
2 tablespoons black sesame seeds

LEMON AND WHITE WINE VINEGAR DRESSING
¼ cup extra virgin olive oil
1 tablespoon lemon juice
2 tablespoons white wine vinegar or balsamic vinegar
2 teaspoons Dijon mustard

Remove the peels from the oranges with a sharp knife and cut the fruit horizontally into slices, discarding any seeds. Combine in a bowl with the fennel, onion, spinach, salmon, and beans, then transfer to a serving platter.

To make the dressing, place all the ingredients in a glass jar with a lid and shake well. Drizzle over the salad and finish with a sprinkling of sesame seeds.

---

488 calories; 30 g protein; 38 g carb; 26 g fat; 2 g saturated fat; 60 mg cholesterol; 11 g fiber; 310 mg sodium

If I'm serving this for a special lunch or dinner, I usually buy some fresh salmon and bake it myself. Place a 7- to 8-ounce piece of salmon fillet in a baking dish and bake in a preheated 350°F oven for 15 to 20 minutes or until just cooked. Drizzle the salmon with a mixture of ¼ cup orange juice, a little olive oil, and a dash of balsamic vinegar and proceed with the recipe as above.

Salmon, Beet and Goat Cheese Salad

This is lovely with canned salmon, but for a special lunch or dinner I often use baked or grilled salmon and finish with a handful of caramelized walnuts (page 140).

Serves 4 | Prep time: 15 minutes | Cooking time: 10 minutes

8 to 10 baby beets, stems trimmed to ½ inch, very well washed and scrubbed
¼ cup pine nuts or crushed walnuts
One 14-ounce can red salmon, drained, bones removed, flesh crumbled
½ salad onion, finely sliced
½ cup roughly chopped flat-leaf parsley
6 pieces sun-dried tomato, finely sliced (or use 12 cherry tomatoes, halved)
6 cups baby spinach or mixed baby salad leaves
¼ cup soft goat cheese or feta marinated in olive oil
1 to 2 tablespoons vincotto or aged balsamic vinegar
1 tablespoon lemon juice
Flaky sea salt and freshly ground black pepper to taste

Steam or microwave the beets for 5 to 7 minutes or until tender. Allow to cool slightly, then run under cold water while you remove the skin. Slice into quarters or in half if very small.

Place the nuts in a nonstick frying pan and toast over medium heat, shaking constantly, until the nuts are golden. Keep an eye on them as they can burn easily.

Combine the beets, salmon, onion, parsley, tomato, and spinach in a large serving bowl. (If using cooked salmon, let it cool first before adding it to the rest of the salad.) Crumble the cheese over the top and sprinkle with the toasted nuts. Drizzle with the vincotto and lemon juice, season with salt and pepper, and serve.

---

303 calories; 27 g protein; 23 g carb; 12 g fat; 4 g saturated fat; 43 mg cholesterol; 7 g fiber; 814 mg sodium

If you are going to leave the tops on your beets, you must wash them very well, as there is nothing worse than that crunch from missed grit! To be on the safe side, I generally trim the tops.

If you like, replace the parsley with dill or add a bunch of lightly steamed asparagus spears.

Smoked Trout and Celeriac Salad with Poppy-Seed Dressing

The celeriac, lemon juice, and vinegar cut through the richness of the smoked trout. When celeriac is out of season, use any combination of shredded cabbage, radishes, cucumbers, and sliced celery.

Gently combine all the salad ingredients except the salt and pepper in a large bowl.

To make the dressing, place all the ingredients in a glass jar with a lid and shake well. Drizzle the dressing over the salad and gently toss to coat. Season with salt and pepper. Transfer to a platter, if desired, and serve.

This is not the sliced smoked ocean trout that is similar in appearance to sliced smoked salmon. You can purchase the trout boned and flavored in cryovac portions of about 3 to 4 ounces from the supermarket or whole from your local fishmonger and some supermarkets.

Add flavor and texture to the salad with some crispy prosciutto. Heat a small nonstick frying pan over medium heat and lightly spray with oil. Add 2 slices of prosciutto and cook for 1 to 2 minutes on each side or until crispy. Remove from the heat and cool, then tear into strips and scatter over the salad.

SERVES 4

Prep time: 15 minutes

12 ounces smoked trout, gently removed from bones and flaked

6 cups arugula

12 ounces celeriac, shredded (4 cups)

½ cup roughly chopped dill

1 avocado, sliced

6 pieces sun-dried tomato, finely sliced

Flaky sea salt and freshly ground black pepper to taste

POPPY-SEED DRESSING

3 tablespoons extra virgin olive oil

1 tablespoon lemon juice

1 tablespoon white wine vinegar or verjuice

1 teaspoon Dijon mustard

1 tablespoon poppy seeds

455 calories, 33 g protein, 14 g carb, 30 g fat; 3 g saturated fat; 88 mg cholesterol; 5 g fiber; 620 mg sodium

Tuna, Green Beans and Caper Salad

Heating the chickpeas or beans is optional, but I like to do this when using them in a salad as the warmth helps diffuse the flavors.

Serves 4 | Prep time: 10 minutes | Cooking time: 10 minutes

5 ounces baby green beans, topped not tailed
1 ear corn
2 large eggs
Olive oil
1 cup canned chickpeas, cannellini beans, or soybeans, rinsed and drained
Three 5-ounce cans tuna in oil, drained
2 tablespoons capers or chopped cornichons
6 cups baby spinach
Flaky sea salt and freshly ground black pepper to taste
Lemon wedges

LEMON AND WHITE WINE VINEGAR DRESSING
¼ cup extra virgin olive oil
1 tablespoon lemon juice
2 tablespoons white wine vinegar or balsamic vinegar
2 teaspoons Dijon mustard

Steam the beans and corn, or place in a small saucepan with a little water and boil for 2 to 3 minutes or until the beans are just cooked. Immediately plunge into ice-cold water to refresh and stop the cooking process. Drain. Using a sharp knife, cut the kernels off the cob in long strips.

Place the eggs in a small saucepan of water and bring to a boil. Cook for 2 minutes from the time when it boils, then place the eggs in cold water for a few minutes. When cool enough to handle, peel and gently slice into quarters.

Heat the same saucepan over medium heat. Add a drizzle of olive oil and the chickpeas and toss for 2 minutes. Remove from the heat.

Meanwhile, to make the dressing, place all the ingredients in a glass jar with a lid and shake well.

Combine the beans and corn, eggs, chickpeas, and the remaining salad ingredients in a bowl, add the dressing, and gently toss to coat. Season with salt and pepper and serve on a large platter with lemon wedges.

467 calories; 34 g protein; 22 g carb; 35 g fat; 5 g saturated fat; 163 mg cholesterol; 66g fiber; 1105 mg sodium

Tuna, Red Pepper and Avocado Salad   >

Another great salad staple of mine. For an even quicker version, use three well-drained 5-ounce cans of tuna in oil instead of the fresh steaks.

Serves 4 | Prep time: 15 minutes

1 pound tuna steaks
Extra virgin olive oil, for brushing and drizzling
1 red bell pepper, finely chopped
1 red onion, sliced
2 celery stalks, sliced on the diagonal
¾ cup roughly chopped mint
1 firm ripe avocado, cut into cubes
2 small cucumbers, sliced on the diagonal
12 cherry tomatoes
One 15-ounce can chickpeas, rinsed and drained
6 cups arugula, baby spinach, or small-leaf salad mix
3 tablespoons apple balsamic vinegar
Flaky sea salt and freshly ground black pepper to taste

Brush the tuna steaks with a little oil and cook in a nonstick grill pan for 3 to 4 minutes on each side or until cooked to your liking. Set aside to rest.

Place the pepper, onion, celery, mint, avocado, cucumbers, cherry tomatoes, chickpeas, and salad leaves in a bowl and toss gently to combine.

Slice the tuna and arrange over the salad, then finish with a good drizzle of apple balsamic and olive oil. Season with salt and pepper and serve.

385 calories; 35 g protein; 35 g carb; 13 g fat; 2 g saturated fat; 51 mg cholesterol; 11 g fiber; 449 mg sodium

Replace the red pepper with 4 marinated artichokes, drained and sliced into quarters (the baby variety has a great look and taste) or a bunch of baby beets, steamed (or use canned).

If apple balsamic vinegar is not available, mix together 2 tablespoons balsamic vinegar and 2 tablespoons apple juice concentrate.

≡ Quinoa is low GI and full of protein and fiber—a very versatile seed that can be substituted for other grains and legumes.

Seared Chicken, Mango and Quinoa Salad

This is a great summer salad when mangoes are in season. If you have the grill cranked up, use it to sear the chicken slices—it lends a deliciously smoky flavor to the salad.

Rinse the quinoa several times then place in a small saucepan and cover with the stock. Bring to a boil, then reduce the heat and simmer for 10 minutes or until the quinoa is tender and translucent. Drain and set aside.

Meanwhile, heat a nonstick frying pan or grill pan over medium heat. When hot, spray with oil, then add the chicken and cook for 2 to 3 minutes on each side or until cooked through. Remove from the heat and rest for 5 minutes or so before finely slicing or shredding.

To make the dressing, place all the ingredients in a glass jar with a lid and shake well. Pour half the dressing over the chicken pieces and toss to coat.

Combine the quinoa, chicken, and the remaining salad ingredients in a bowl and drizzle with the remaining dressing. Transfer to a large platter to serve, if you like.

> If you're running short on time, buy a roasted free-range chicken from a supermarket or deli, remove the skin, and shred the meat into the salad.

SERVES 4
Prep time: 20 minutes
Cooking time: 10 minutes

1 cup quinoa
2 cups chicken stock or water
Olive oil spray
3 boneless, skinless chicken breasts, cut into 1-inch slices
2 celery stalks, sliced on the diagonal
2 scallions, sliced on the diagonal
1 mango, sliced
1 avocado, sliced
6 cups mixed baby green leaves
½ cup chopped or torn basil and/ or mint

GRAINY MUSTARD AND APPLE BALSAMIC DRESSING
2 tablespoons apple balsamic vinegar, or 1 tablespoon each balsamic vinegar and apple juice concentrate
1 tablespoon lemon juice
2 tablespoons olive oil
2 teaspoons grainy mustard
Flaky sea salt and freshly ground black pepper to taste

---

427 calories; 21 g protein; 48 g carb; 19 g fat; 2 g saturated fat; 33 mg cholesterol; 8 g fiber; 271 mg sodium

Shredded Turkey, Apple and Almond Slaw

The freshness of the mint and sweetness of the apple make this a delicious summer salad. Try it with smoked chicken instead of turkey.

Serves 2 | Prep time: 10 minutes | Cooking time: 10 minutes

½ cup slivered almonds
8 ounces shredded or finely sliced turkey breast
2 cups finely shredded Chinese cabbage or celeriac
1 red apple, grated or shredded
½ red onion, finely sliced
Flaky sea salt to taste
¾ cup finely sliced or roughly torn mint

CREAMY YOGURT DRESSING
3 tablespoons low-fat plain yogurt
2 tablespoons white wine vinegar
2 tablespoons finely chopped chervil or dill, optional

Preheat the oven to 400°F and line a baking sheet with parchment paper. Spread out the almonds on the sheet and bake for 7 to 10 minutes or until golden (alternatively, toss them in a nonstick frying pan over medium heat for a few minutes).

Meanwhile, to make the dressing, place all the ingredients in a glass jar with a lid and shake well.

Combine all the salad ingredients in a bowl, add the dressing, and toss gently to coat.

467 calories; 43 g protein; 28 g carb; 27 g fat; 2 g saturated fat; 80 mg cholesterol; 7 g fiber; 385 mg sodium)

> If you have some dry-roasted almonds in the fridge, crush them in a mortar and pestle and use these instead of the slivered almonds.

Turkey, Pear and Walnut Salad with a Dill Yogurt Dressing >

This is my low-GI take on a Waldorf salad. It also works beautifully with shredded poached chicken or even a purchased roast chicken (remove the skin first).

Serves 4 | Prep time: 15 minutes

CREAMY YOGURT AND DILL DRESSING
¼ cup low-fat plain yogurt
¼ cup mayonnaise
1 tablespoon lemon juice or apple cider vinegar
2 tablespoons roughly chopped dill

1 pound shaved turkey, roughly chopped
2 pears, preferably bosc, finely sliced
1 English cucumber, peeled, cut in half lengthwise, seeded, and thinly sliced
4 celery stalks, sliced thinly on the diagonal
¾ cup chopped dill
6 cups butter lettuce, mâche, or baby romaine (or a combination)
¼ cup lightly crushed walnuts or roasted almonds

To make the dressing, place all the ingredients in a glass jar with a lid and shake well.

Place the turkey, pears, cucumber, celery, dill, and lettuce in a bowl, drizzle with the dressing, and toss gently to combine. Sprinkle the nuts over the top and serve.

410 calories; 36 g protein; 24 g carb; 25 g fat; 3 g saturated fat; 91 mg cholesterol; 5 g fiber; 209 mg sodium

> You can purchase your shaved turkey from your supermarket or local deli—a wonderful, lean protein ready for action.

Moroccan Lamb with Chickpeas and Spinach

SERVES 4

Prep time: 10 minutes

Cooking time: 10 minutes

1 pound lamb tenderloin

¼ cup *dukkah* (see box)

Olive oil spray

5 ounces baby green beans, topped not tailed

One 15-ounce can chickpeas or cannellini beans, rinsed and drained

7 ounces cherry tomatoes or baby grape tomatoes, halved

3 cups baby spinach

3 cups finely sliced radicchio

1 tablespoon white balsamic vinegar or verjuice

1 tablespoon lemon olive oil

¼ cup soft goat cheese or feta marinated in olive oil

---

528 calories; 30 g protein; 25 g carb; 34 g fat; 13 g saturated fat; 88 mg cholesterol; 7 g fiber; 637 mg sodium

Dukkah is a delicious and very versatile spice and nut mixture. It is great as a coating for lamb, turkey, chicken, and fish, sprinkled on salads and steamed vegetables with a little extra virgin olive oil, and over the Cauliflower and Celeriac Soup (page 57) and the Moroccan Cabbage, Cannellini Bean and Cilantro Soup (page 53). The recipe for *dukkah* below makes more than a cup, but it lasts for weeks in the fridge—if you can keep this Moorish combination that long!

Roll the lamb in the *dukkah*, firmly pressing the spice mix onto the meat. Heat a non-stick frying pan over medium heat. When hot, spray with oil, then add the lamb and cook for 3 to 4 minutes on each side or until medium-rare. Remove from the pan and rest for 10 minutes before slicing.

Meanwhile, steam the baby green beans or place them in a shallow frying pan of boiling water and simmer for 3 to 4 minutes or until just tender. Remove and plunge into ice-cold water to refresh and stop the cooking process. Drain.

Combine the sliced lamb, baby green beans, chickpeas, tomatoes, spinach, and radicchio in a bowl. Drizzle with the vinegar and oil and toss to coat. Transfer to a platter, if you like, crumble the cheese over the top, and serve.

Cut some sweet potato into ¾-inch pieces, lightly spray with oil, and roast until golden. Toss through the salad just before serving. It's also delicious with roasted beets.

Dress up the salad with a sprinkling of dried currants, pomegranate seeds, or toasted pine nuts.

To make the *dukkah*, preheat the oven to 350°F. Place ⅓ cup hazelnuts on a baking sheet and bake for 6 to 8 minutes or until lightly toasted. Remove from the oven, wrap the nuts in a tea towel, and gently rub them together to remove the skins. Meanwhile, toast ⅓ cup slivered almonds, ⅓ cup sesame seeds, and 2 tablespoons coriander seeds in a nonstick frying pan over medium heat, shaking the pan frequently, for 4 to 5 minutes or until lightly golden. Place all the nuts and seeds in a food processor along with 2 tablespoons cumin, 2 teaspoons flaky sea salt, and 1 teaspoon freshly ground black pepper and process until roughly chopped. (You may use a mortar and pestle instead.)

≡ Pure maple syrup or honey may be used instead of the juice concentrate in the dressing.

Beef, Prosciutto and Sweet Potato Salad

Delicious and nourishing all in one. The vitamin C from the sweet potatoes and tomatoes will help your body absorb the iron from the beef.

Preheat the oven to 350°F. Line two baking sheets with parchment paper.

Spray the sweet potatoes with a little oil, sprinkle with salt, and toss. Arrange on one of the sheets in a single layer and bake for 30 minutes or until lightly golden. Place the prosciutto on the other sheet and bake for 5 to 7 minutes or until crisp. Remove both sheets from the oven and drain the prosciutto on paper towels.

Meanwhile, season the beef with salt and pepper. Heat a grill pan over medium-high heat, lightly spray with oil, then add the beef and cook for 3 to 4 minutes on each side (or longer, according to taste). Remove from the heat and let the beef rest in the pan for 5 to 10 minutes. Cut into slices.

While the beef rests, place all the dressing ingredients in a glass jar with a lid and shake well.

Arrange the salad leaves, sweet potatoes, beef, prosciutto, radishes, and tomatoes on a platter. Drizzle the dressing over the top, toss well, and sprinkle with the chives, if using.

Instead of sweet potatoes, use Jerusalem artichokes for a delicious nutty variation. The baking time will depend on the thickness of the slices. If you use a mandoline, you will only need to bake for 10 to 12 minutes in a preheated 360°F oven; if the slices are thicker (about ¼ inch), increase the cooking time to 30 to 35 minutes.

Kid Friendly I suspect most kids would prefer this salad without the radishes.

SERVES 4 TO 6
Prep time: 15 minutes
Cooking time: 40 minutes

1 pound baby sweet potatoes, cut into ¼-inch slices
Olive oil spray
Flaky sea salt and freshly ground black pepper to taste
8 slices prosciutto
1 pound beef sirloin
8 cups butter lettuce, arugula, or radicchio (or a combination)
4 radishes, finely sliced
8 ounces baby roma or cherry tomatoes, halved
3 tablespoons chopped chives, optional

FRUITY RED WINE VINEGAR DRESSING
2 tablespoons olive oil or lemon olive oil
1 tablespoon red wine vinegar
1 teaspoon Dijon mustard
1 teaspoon pear or apple juice concentrate

523 calories; 33 g protein; 33 g carb; 29 g fat; 8 g saturated fat; 91 mg cholesterol; 5 g fiber; 980 mg sodium

Main Meals
with Fish

The beauty of cooking a meal with fish is that it generally comes together pretty quickly—perfect for busy weeknight dinners. Whether you choose to bake, grill, or poach your seafood or simmer it in a curry, the recipes on the following pages offer something for everyone.

Ricotta and Basil Battered Fish with Baby Carrots

SERVES 4

Prep time: 10 minutes

Cooking time: 5 minutes

2 large eggs

4 to 5 tablespoons low-fat ricotta

½ cup finely chopped basil

8 ounces baby carrots, trimmed,
   leaving ½-inch green tops

Broccoli with Lemon Olive Oil and
   Parmesan (page 143)

1 to 2 tablespoons olive oil

1½ pounds flounder or tilapia fillets

Lemon wedges

---

355 calories; 43 g protein; 12 g carb; 13 g
fat; 2 g saturated fat; 194 mg cholesterol;
5 g fiber; 272 mg sodium

An excellent source of lean protein, freshly caught fish makes a regular appearance in our home. The delicate herb batter coats mild fish fillets without masking their flavor.

Whisk together the eggs, ricotta, and basil to make a batter.

Place the baby carrots in a steamer and cook until just tender. Prepare the broccoli.

Meanwhile, heat 1 tablespoon of the oil in a large nonstick frying pan over medium heat. Working in batches so you don't crowd the pan, immerse the fish fillets in the batter, then place them in the pan and cook for 1 to 2 minutes on each side or until cooked. Remove and drain on paper towels. Add more oil if required.

Stack the fillets in the center of each plate and serve with the steamed carrots, broccoli, and lemon wedges.

If the fillets are large, cut them into 4- to 6-inch pieces. They are easier to turn in the pan and look great stacked on the plate.

This dish is also delicious with Cauliflower and White Bean Puree (page 148) or sweet potato and celeriac fries (page 146).

≡ As an alternative to the carrots and broccoli, a trio of fresh corn, baby green beans, and carrots makes a lovely side dish for the fish.

Coconut and Lime Fish Curry with Fresh Spinach

SERVES 4
Prep time: 20 minutes
Cooking time: 10 minutes

1½ pounds firm white fish fillets (such as cod, tilapia, or snapper), cut into large pieces
Juice of 2 limes (or the juice of 1 lemon)
One 14-ounce can light coconut milk
1 cup light evaporated milk
4 scallions, cut in half
1 small red chile, seeded and finely chopped
2 tablespoons finely chopped lemongrass
2 kaffir lime leaves
1 tablespoon fish sauce
2 tablespoons ground almonds
¾ cup roughly chopped cilantro, plus extra to garnish
9 cups baby spinach
2 cups steamed basmati rice
¼ cup fried shallots (page 14), optional

391 calories; 42 g protein; 50 g carb; 8 g fat; 5 g saturated fat; 76 mg cholesterol; 4 g fiber; 623 mg sodium

This is a very mild curry and great for kids. If you want to spice it up, simply add some more finely chopped red chile.

Place the fish pieces in a bowl and squeeze the lime juice over the top.

Combine the coconut milk, evaporated milk, scallions, chile, lemongrass, lime leaves, fish sauce, and ground almonds in a large saucepan, then cover and bring to a simmer. Gently stir in the cilantro, fish pieces, and lime juice and simmer for 6 to 7 minutes or until the fish is just cooked. Add the spinach and put the lid back on until it has collapsed (this should take only 2 to 3 minutes).

To serve, place a small amount of rice in each bowl and ladle the curry over the top. Garnish with the fried shallots, if using, and a little extra cilantro.

Read the labels carefully when buying coconut milk or cream—often a reduced-fat coconut cream will have less fat than another brand's coconut milk. If fat is not an issue, use regular coconut milk.

If you like, replace the spinach with steamed bok choy or choy sum and serve with steamed green beans. Or you can cook the beans by adding them to the curry a few minutes prior to serving.

Add a handful of roughly torn basil instead of the lemongrass, if desired.

Try mandarin, mango, or grapefruit segments instead of orange in the salad, and replace the snow peas with asparagus.

Snapper with Pomegranate, Soy and Maple Syrup Dressing

We all love this dish, with its tangy dressing and sweet salad. Sprinkle flat-leaf parsley, mint, cilantro, or chervil over the salad, if you like.

Serves 4 | Prep time: 15 minutes | Cooking time: 10 minutes

POMEGRANATE, SOY AND MAPLE SYRUP DRESSING
1 tablespoon pure maple syrup
2 tablespoons low-sodium tamari or soy sauce
2 teaspoons pomegranate molasses or lemon juice
¼ cup chicken stock

1 tablespoon olive oil
Four 7-ounce snapper fillets
Snow pea, Avocado and Orange Salad (page 143)
Flaky sea salt and freshly ground black pepper to taste

To make the dressing, place all the ingredients in a glass jar with a lid and shake well.

Heat the oil in a nonstick frying pan over high heat and add the fish fillets, skin-side down. Reduce the heat to medium and cook for 2 to 3 minutes, then turn and cook the other side for 2 to 3 minutes. Remove and keep warm.

Add the dressing to the pan and bring to a boil.

To serve, spoon the salad into the center of four plates, place the fish on top, and drizzle with the warm dressing. Season with salt and pepper.

394 calories; 39 g protein; 20 g carb; 18 g fat; 2 g saturated fat; 63 mg cholesterol; 5 g fiber; 514 mg sodium

Baked Cod with Baby Spinach and Cherry Tomatoes

This incredibly simple dish takes just minutes to prepare, leaving you free to relax and unwind as it bakes.

Serves 4 | Prep time: 10 minutes | Cooking time: 25 minutes

Olive oil spray
10 ounces baby spinach
1 salad onion, finely sliced
16 kalamata olives, pitted and sliced lengthwise
7 ounces grape or cherry tomatoes, cut in half
8 sprigs thyme, plus extra sprigs to garnish
1½ pounds firm white fish fillets, such as cod or haddock
1 cup chicken stock
Olive oil, for drizzling
Flaky sea salt and freshly ground black pepper to taste
2 cups steamed basmati rice

Preheat the oven to 400°F. Lightly spray a nonstick baking dish with oil.

Place the spinach in the dish and layer the onion, olives, tomatoes, and half the thyme over the top. Arrange the fish fillets over the vegetables, add the stock, and drizzle with a little olive oil. Season with salt and pepper, then cover with parchment paper and bake for 20 to 25 minutes or until the fish is cooked.

To serve, spoon a little rice onto each plate, ladle the vegetables over the rice, and gently place the fish fillets on top. Garnish with extra thyme sprigs.

336 calories; 36 g protein; 44 g carb; 8 g fat; 0 g saturated fat; 74 mg cholesterol; 4 g fiber; 530 mg sodium

Replace the thyme with rosemary for a subtle change in flavor.

≡ Add finely chopped lemongrass root to the stock for extra flavor. Garnish with snow pea sprouts, if you like.

‹ Baked Salmon in Ginger and Soy with Sugar Snaps

The fish parcels are also delicious served over Buttered Cabbage (page 144) or with steamed Asian greens, tossed in oyster or hoisin sauce.

Serves 4 | Prep time: 10 minutes | Cooking time: 20 minutes

About ½ cup chicken stock
2 to 3 tablespoons grated ginger
4 nori sheets
Four 7-ounce salmon fillets
2 tablespoons low-sodium tamari or soy sauce
1 pound sugar snap peas or snow peas, topped and tailed
2 cups steamed basmati rice

Preheat the oven to 350°F. Pour the stock into a medium nonstick baking dish to a depth of about ¾ inch and add 1 tablespoon of the ginger.

Place the nori sheets on a flat surface, shiny-side down. Spread the remaining ginger over the top side of the salmon fillets and place, skin-side up, in the center of the nori sheets. Fold to make a neat parcel. Place the parcels in the stock, seam-side down, and drizzle with the tamari. Cover loosely with parchment paper and bake for 15 minutes for medium-rare or 20 minutes for medium.

Just prior to serving, steam the peas until just tender.

To serve, spoon a little rice into the center of four plates. Using a razor-sharp knife, trim the ends of the salmon parcels (keep them for a snack the next day). Carefully slice each piece of salmon in half on the diagonal. Place the fish on the rice and the peas to the side. Ladle the gingery stock over the top and serve.

436 calories; 51 g protein; 43 g carb; 12 g fat; 3 g saturated fat; 91 mg cholesterol; 4 g fiber; 405 mg sodium

Nori sheets are made from seaweed and are a fantastic source of zinc and antioxidants. They're available from Asian food stores and the Asian section of larger supermarkets. However, some palates may find their flavor a little strong—if this is the case, leave out the nori and place the salmon and ginger in the stock. Proceed with the recipe.

Poached Salmon with Fennel and Asparagus

This dish is fresh, light, and luxurious all at the same time, and seems to appeal to everyone.

Serves 4 | Prep time: 10 minutes | Cooking time: 20 minutes

Olive oil spray
1 large fennel bulb, finely sliced (reserve the fronds for garnish)
2 cups chicken stock
3 scallions, finely sliced on the diagonal
1 tablespoon grated ginger
Four 7-ounce salmon fillets
16 asparagus spears
Cauliflower and White Bean Puree (page 148)

Heat a large nonstick frying pan over medium heat and spray well with oil. Add the fennel and cook for 5 to 6 minutes or until softened. Increase the heat, add the stock, scallions, and ginger, and cook for 2 to 3 minutes. Reduce the heat to a simmer and move the fennel to the side. Gently place the salmon fillets in the pan and cook, covered, for 5 minutes or until the salmon is cooked to your liking.

Meanwhile, snap the ends off the asparagus spears and lightly steam, then plunge into cold water to refresh and stop the cooking. Leave the spears whole or cut them into thirds on the diagonal.

Remove the cooked salmon from the pan and keep warm. Increase the heat, add the asparagus, and cook for 1 to 2 minutes or until warmed through.

To serve, divide the Cauliflower and White Bean Puree among four plates and top with the salmon, asparagus and sliced fennel. Spoon over the stock and garnish with the reserved fennel fronds.

493 calories; 54 g protein; 35 g carb; 15 g fat; 4 g saturated fat; 97 mg cholesterol; 13 g fiber; 587 mg sodium

A small serving of steamed basmati rice is delicious with this dish instead of the puree.

Sauteed Salmon on Orange Lentils

I love these orange-flavored lentils and also serve them as a warm side with chicken, fish, or lamb. They have it all: They're low GI, high in flavor and protein, and my kids love them!

SERVES 4
Prep time: 20 minutes
Cooking time: 30 minutes

3 tablespoons white wine or verjuice
2 tablespoons lemon juice
Flaky sea salt and freshly ground
    black pepper to taste
Four 7-ounce salmon steaks
Olive oil spray

ORANGE LENTILS

½ cup puy-style lentils, rinsed and
    drained
Chicken stock, to cover
1 tablespoon olive oil
1 onion, finely chopped
½ red bell pepper, finely chopped
½ celery stalk, finely chopped
1 carrot, finely chopped
2 garlic cloves, finely chopped
½ cup fresh orange juice
Grated zest of 1 orange

APPLE BALSAMIC GLAZE

2 tablespoons apple balsamic
    vinegar, or 1 tablespoon each
    balsamic vinegar and apple juice
    concentrate
2 tablespoons olive oil or lemon olive
    oil
1 tablespoon lemon juice

---

515 calories; 51 g protein; 25 g carb; 23 g fat; 3 g saturated fat; 89 mg cholesterol; 9 g fiber; 222 mg sodium

Combine the white wine, lemon juice, and salt and pepper in a nonmetallic bowl, add the salmon, and turn to coat. Cover and refrigerate while you cook the lentils.

To make the orange lentils, place the lentils in a saucepan and cover with stock. Bring to a boil, then reduce the heat and simmer for 10 to 15 minutes or until tender. Drain and set aside.

Heat the oil in another saucepan over medium-high heat and cook the onion, red pepper, celery, and carrot for 8 to 10 minutes until softened. Add the garlic, drained lentils, orange juice, and most of the orange zest (reserve a little to garnish) and stir well. Reduce the heat to medium–low and cook gently while you prepare the salmon, adding more stock if required.

Remove the salmon from the marinade. Heat a nonstick frying pan over medium-high heat, spray well with oil, and add the salmon. Cook for 2 to 3 minutes on each side or longer, according to taste.

Meanwhile, to make the apple balsamic glaze, place all the ingredients in a glass jar with a lid and shake well. Gently warm through in a small saucepan.

To serve, ladle the lentils into the center of four plates, place the salmon on top, and drizzle with the warm glaze. Sprinkle with the reserved orange zest.

Try serving the salmon on Snow Pea, Avocado and Orange Salad (page 143). Or replace the lentils with well-rinsed quinoa.

Sometimes I stir in a teaspoon each of cumin and pomegranate molasses when adding the garlic.

Whiting with Lemon and Almond Crumble

SERVES 4
Prep time: 10 minutes
Cooking time: 5 minutes

½ cup slivered almonds
¼ cup grated lemon zest
¼ cup finely chopped flat-leaf parsley
2 garlic cloves, finely chopped
Flaky sea salt and freshly ground
    black pepper to taste
Olive oil spray
1½ tablespoons butter
1½ pounds whiting fillets
Shredded Celeriac with Fennel Seeds
    (page 148)
Lemon wedges

Green salad

---

539 calories; 39 g protein; 26 g carb; 33 g fat; 4 g saturated fat; 126 mg cholesterol; 7 g fiber; 678 mg sodium

The zesty, crunchy topping goes wonderfully with most types of fish fillets, such as cod, flounder, or haddock.

Mix together the almonds, lemon zest, parsley, garlic, and salt and pepper on a plate.

Heat a small nonstick frying pan over medium–low heat. Spray well with oil and, when hot, add the almond and lemon mixture. Cook for 1 to 2 minutes or until golden, then remove from the pan.

Heat a large nonstick frying pan over medium heat. When hot, add the butter and spray well with oil. Gently place the fish in the pan, skin-side down, and cook for 1 to 2 minutes on each side.

Sprinkle the lemon and almond mixture over the fish and serve with Shredded Celeriac with Fennel Seeds, lemon wedges, and a fresh green salad.

Vary the flavors in the crumble—for example, use sesame seeds or ground almonds instead of slivered almonds, and basil instead of parsley.

When celeriac is out of season or you are feeding a younger crowd, try serving the fish with Cauliflower Bake (page 144) instead.

Lemon and Herb-Crusted Tuna with Baby Green Beans

Tuna is an excellent source of high-quality protein and omega-3 fats, and is delicious with the bright taste of fresh herbs, olives, and apple balsamic dressing.

Serves 4 | Prep time: 15 minutes | Cooking time: 10 minutes

APPLE BALSAMIC DRESSING
2 tablespoons apple balsamic vinegar, or 1 tablespoon
    each balsamic vinegar and apple juice concentrate
2 tablespoons olive oil or lemon olive oil
2 tablespoons lemon juice

¼ cup grated lemon zest
½ cup finely chopped flat-leaf parsley
½ cup finely chopped basil
1 teaspoon each freshly ground black pepper and flaky
    sea salt
Four 7-ounce tuna fillets (about 1 inch thick)
Lemon olive oil, for brushing
5 ounces baby green beans, topped not tailed
20 kalamata olives, pitted
9 cups baby spinach or arugula
12 cherry tomatoes, cut in half
2 cucumbers, seeded and sliced

To make the dressing, place all the ingredients in a glass jar with a lid and shake well.

Combine the lemon zest, parsley, basil, salt, and pepper, then press the mixture onto the tuna steaks.

Heat a nonstick frying pan over high heat. When hot, brush with oil, then add the steaks. Reduce the heat to medium and cook for 1 to 2 minutes on each side.

Lightly steam the beans, then plunge into cold water to refresh and stop the cooking process. Drain and set aside.

Remove the tuna from the pan and place on a cutting board. Cut into ½-inch slices.

Heat the same frying pan over medium-high heat and add the olives. Flatten with a spatula then pour in the dressing and cook gently for 1 to 2 minutes.

To serve, place the spinach on a large platter and scatter the beans, tomato halves, tuna, and cucumbers over the top. Pour the warm dressing and olives over the salad.

---

418 calories; 50 g protein; 19 g carb; 16 g fat; 2 g saturated fat; 89 mg cholesterol; 7 g fiber; 400 mg sodium

Baked Peppers with Tuna and Ricotta >

The recipe makes twice as much tuna mixture as you'll need to stuff the peppers, but this is no problem: For dinner the next night, toss it with rigatoni or spiral noodles, sprinkle with mozzarella, and bake until golden.

Serves 4 | Prep time: 20 minutes | Cooking time: 45 minutes

4 yellow or red bell peppers, halved lengthwise and seeded
1 tablespoon olive oil
1½ celery stalks, finely chopped
1 white onion, finely chopped
1 large carrot, grated or shredded
2 cups tomato passata or tomato sauce
½ cup tomato paste
3 cups chicken stock
Six 5-ounce cans tuna in olive oil, drained
¾ cup roughly chopped flat-leaf parsley
4 garlic cloves, finely chopped
3 tablespoons low-fat ricotta
3 tablespoons shaved or grated Parmesan

Green salad

Preheat the oven to 350°F.

Place the peppers, cut-side up, in a small glass or ceramic baking dish. Bake for 15 minutes. Mop up any liquid in the base of the dish with paper towels.

Meanwhile, heat the oil in a large saucepan over medium heat and cook the celery, onion, and carrot for 4 to 5 minutes or until softened. Add the tomato passata, tomato paste, and 2½ cups stock and cook for another 4 to 5 minutes. Add the tuna, parsley, and garlic and cook over high heat for 5 minutes, stirring regularly.

Remove the peppers from the oven. Spoon the tuna mixture into the peppers, top with a dollop of ricotta and a sprinkling of Parmesan. Pour the remaining stock into the base of the dish and bake for another 25 to 30 minutes.

Serve with a green salad.

---

539 calories; 35 g protein; 26 g carb; 37 g fat; 3 g saturated fat; 54 mg cholesterol; 6 g fiber; 786 mg sodium

≡ Longer cooking will intensify the flavor—add extra stock to the baking dish so the peppers don't dry out.

Baked Trout in Grape Leaves with Warm Eggplant and Red Pepper Salsa

While this is a favorite of mine, I do understand that some people may not like the strong flavor grape leaves bring to a dish. It's fine to leave them out and cover with parchment paper instead.

Preheat the oven to 350°F.

Place each piece of fish, skin-side down, in the center of a grape leaf and fold the leaf over. If the leaves are small, use another one to at least surround the middle of the fish pieces. Place the fish parcels in a baking dish and pour the stock over the top. Bake for 20 to 25 minutes.

To serve, spoon some salsa into the center of each plate, then place the fish on top and sprinkle with pine nuts.

I buy grape leaves in brine in a jar. Once opened, store them in the fridge where they will last for months. Rinse off the salty brine and pat the leaves dry before use.

This is delicious with some crumbled feta or a dollop of tzatziki or plain yogurt over the fish.

SERVES 4
Prep time: 10 minutes
Cooking time: 25 minutes

Four 7-ounce rainbow trout fillets
4 to 8 grape leaves in brine (depending on size)
½ cup chicken stock
Warm Eggplant and Red Pepper Salsa (page 149)
2 tablespoons toasted pine nuts

515 calories; 45 g protein; 35 g carb; 22 g fat; 3 g saturated fat; 165 mg cholesterol; 11 g fiber; 561 mg sodium

Main Meals
with Chicken

To me, a tender, lightly grilled chicken breast is one of the simple pleasures in life, and an excellent source of protein. But I also enjoy slow-cooking chicken, giving it plenty of time to absorb the flavors around it. Chicken tagine is a particular favorite, and perfectly illustrates how a few well-chosen ingredients can come together to create a really special dish.

Chicken and Apple Balls in Tomato and Red Pepper Sauce

SERVES 4 TO 6
Prep time: 30 minutes
Cooking time: 1 hour

1 tablespoon olive oil
1 onion, finely chopped
1 large red bell pepper, finely chopped
Two 14.5-ounce cans diced tomatoes
2 cups tomato passata or tomato
    sauce
½ cup tomato paste
4 cups chicken stock
Flaky sea salt to taste
¾ cup roughly chopped flat-leaf
    parsley
4 garlic cloves, finely chopped
6 cups baby spinach

CHICKEN AND APPLE BALLS
1¼ pounds lean ground chicken (or
    use ground turkey, pork, or veal)
3 tablespoons natural oat bran or
    ground almonds
1 zucchini or carrot, grated or
    shredded
1 apple, grated or shredded
1 tablespoon tomato paste
1 to 1½ tablespoons apple juice
    concentrate
½ cup finely chopped flat-leaf parsley
Good pinch of flaky sea salt

417 calories; 44 g protein; 46 g carb; 8 g fat;
1 g saturated fat; 92 mg cholesterol; 11 g
fiber; 523 mg sodium

Another great family dish. As a variation, add the spinach to the sauce 5 minutes prior to serving — you may want to triple the quantity, as cooked spinach collapses into a very small amount.

Heat the oil in a large heavy-bottomed saucepan over medium-high heat and cook the onion and red pepper for 2 to 3 minutes or until the onion has softened but not browned. Add the diced tomatoes, passata, tomato paste, stock, and salt. Bring to a boil, then reduce the heat and simmer for 30 minutes. Stir in the parsley and garlic and simmer for another 30 minutes.

Meanwhile, to make the chicken and apple balls, place all the ingredients in a large mixing bowl and gently combine. Roll the mixture into walnut-sized balls.

About 10 minutes before the end of the sauce's cooking time, gently drop the balls into the liquid and simmer for 10 minutes or until they are cooked through.

To serve, place a handful of spinach in each bowl and ladle the chicken balls and sauce over the top.

Kid Friendly This is great ladled over thick low-GI pasta (such as farfalle, fusilli, linguine, or egg fettuccine), basmati rice, or even mashed sweet potatoes. Finish with a sprinkling of grated Parmesan or shredded mozzarella.

When making the sauce, boost your veggie intake by adding two shredded carrots with the red pepper.

Chicken Tagine with Lemon, Olives and Cilantro

SERVES 4 TO 6
Prep time: 20 minutes
Cooking time: 1¼ hours

1 teaspoon ground cinnamon

2 teaspoons ground ginger or 1 tablespoon grated ginger

2 teaspoons ground cumin

1 teaspoon paprika

1 teaspoon sambal oelek or a good pinch of red pepper flakes, optional

8 bone-in chicken thighs (about 3 pounds), skin removed, or 1¾ pounds boneless, skinless thighs

1 tablespoon olive oil

1 cup chicken stock

4 garlic cloves, crushed or finely chopped

1 large onion, finely chopped

2 tablespoons grated lemon zest, plus extra to garnish

2 tablespoons lemon juice

Flaky sea salt to taste

½ cup puy-style lentils, rinsed and drained

1 cup marinated green olives, pitted and halved

¾ cup roughly chopped flat-leaf parsley

¾ cup roughly chopped cilantro

4 to 6 tablespoons low-fat tzatziki (page 15)

SPINACH SALAD

12 cups baby spinach

1 tablespoon lemon juice

Drizzle of extra virgin olive oil

---

531 calories; 50 g protein; 31 g carb; 23 g fat; 4 g saturated fat; 187 mg cholesterol; 12 g fiber; 887 mg sodium

A tagine is both the name for a Moroccan dish and the conical-shaped vessel it is traditionally cooked in. Please don't worry if you don't have a tagine in your kitchen cupboard—a Dutch oven will work just as well.

Mix together the cinnamon, ginger, cumin, paprika, and sambal oelek and add a little water to make a paste. Spread the spice paste over the chicken pieces.

Heat the oil in a large Dutch oven over medium-high heat. Add the chicken, paste-side down, and cook for 2 to 3 minutes on each side (depending on the size of the dish, you may need to do this in batches). Remove and transfer to a bowl.

Add the stock, garlic, onion, lemon zest, lemon juice, and salt to the pot, mix well, and bring to a gentle simmer. Return the chicken to the pan, paste-side down, then cover and simmer for 30 to 35 minutes. Add the lentils, olives, and parsley and simmer for another 30 minutes. Just prior to serving, stir in the chopped cilantro.

Meanwhile, to make the salad, place the spinach in a bowl, add the lemon juice and olive oil, and toss gently to combine.

To serve, ladle the chicken tagine into large shallow bowls and dollop each serving with a tablespoon of tzatziki and a sprinkling of lemon zest. Serve with the spinach salad.

The lentils are cooked until al dente, but if you prefer them softer add them with the stock. Remember to reduce the heat and use a heat diffuser if you are cooking in a tagine.

This may seem obvious, but I have forgotten enough times to feel it warrants a mention: Zest your lemon before you juice it!

Stir 2 tablespoons finely sliced preserved lemon into the tagine for an authentic touch.

≡ Stir 2 tablespoons finely sliced preserved lemon into the tagine for an authentic touch.

This chicken is also delicious served with Celeriac and Roast Sweet Potato Mash (page 146), or try it with Buttered Cabbage (page 144).

Slow-Baked Chicken with Fennel and Lentils

Add a drained can of cannellini beans instead of lentils for another delicious low-GI meal. Serve with a dollop of low-fat tzatziki or plain yogurt.

Serves 6 | Prep time: 20 minutes | Cooking time: 1 hour

1 tablespoon olive oil
1 onion, sliced or cut into wedges
2 large carrots, sliced
1 large fennel bulb, trimmed and cut into 8 wedges (or use 2 small bulbs)
2 celery stalks, sliced
Olive oil spray
3 pounds bone-in chicken thighs, skin removed
Flaky sea salt and freshly ground black pepper to taste
½ cup white wine or verjuice
2 cups chicken stock
1 teaspoon grainy mustard
½ cup puy-style lentils, rinsed and drained
2 garlic cloves, finely chopped
2 tablespoons low-fat cream cheese
1 to 2 tablespoons finely chopped sage or thyme, plus extra to garnish
3 cups steamed basmati rice

Preheat the oven to 350°F.

Heat the oil in a large Dutch oven over medium-high heat and cook the onion, carrots, fennel, and celery for 4 to 5 minutes or until softened. Remove the vegetables and set aside.

Spray the pot with a little more oil. Season the chicken with salt and pepper, then add to the pot and cook for 1 to 2 minutes on each side. Pour in the wine and stir to deglaze the base, then add the stock and mustard and bring to a boil. Return the vegetables to the dish and add the lentils. Reduce the heat to a gentle simmer and stir in the garlic, cream cheese, and chopped herbs. Cover and bake for 45 minutes. (Alternatively, continue to cook on the stovetop, partially covered, for another 45 minutes, stirring occasionally.)

To serve, spoon some rice into six bowls and ladle the chicken and vegetables over the top. Garnish with extra herbs.

381 calories; 36 g protein; 48 g carb; 9 g fat; 2 g saturated fat; 116 mg cholesterol; 7 g fiber; 297 mg sodium

Poached Ginger Chicken with Buttered Cabbage

There will be plenty of poaching liquid left over. Use it as a base for a chicken and ginger soup the next night, or strain and freeze for a later date.

Serves 4 | Prep time: 20 minutes, plus standing time | Cooking time: 1 hour

One 4-pound chicken, trimmed of excess fat
4 cups chicken stock
One 2½-inch piece ginger, washed and thinly sliced
6 scallions, trimmed and cut in half
6 star anise pods
2 tablespoons low-sodium tamari or soy sauce
2 large handfuls of bean sprouts, optional
Buttered Cabbage (page 144)

GINGER AND CILANTRO SAUCE
2 tablespoons low-sodium tamari or soy sauce
2 tablespoons grated ginger
2 large garlic cloves, crushed
½ to 1 large red chile, finely sliced
1 cup chicken poaching liquid
¾ cup roughly chopped cilantro
2 teaspoons sesame oil

Wash the chicken in cold water and pat dry with paper towels, then place in a large pot, breast-side down. Add the stock, ginger, scallions, star anise, tamari, and 4 cups water. Bring to a boil, then reduce the heat to low and simmer, covered, for 45 minutes. Remove the pan from the heat and rest the chicken in the stock for about 30 minutes.

Meanwhile, if using the bean sprouts, cover them with water and leave to soak for at least 20 minutes. Drain and add to the stock.

To make the ginger and cilantro sauce, combine the tamari, ginger, garlic, chile, and poaching liquid in a small saucepan over medium–low heat and simmer, covered, for 3 to 4 minutes. Just prior to serving, stir in the cilantro and sesame oil.

To serve, remove the chicken from the poaching liquid. Gently peel off and discard the skin and cut the chicken into pieces. Spoon the cabbage onto large plates and arrange the chicken on top. Spoon the bean sprouts, if using, over the chicken and drizzle with the warm sauce.

382 calories; 50 g protein; 18 g carb; 13 g fat; 4 g saturated fat; 155 mg cholesterol; 6 g fiber; 702 mg sodium

Chicken Bolognese in Roasted Peppers with Shredded Parmesan

SERVES 1 (WITH LEFTOVERS)
Prep time: 20 minutes
Cooking time: 1½ hours

4 red bell peppers
1 tablespoon olive oil
1 onion, finely chopped
1½ celery stalks, finely chopped
2 carrots, grated or shredded
Olive oil spray
2 pounds lean ground chicken (or try ground veal, pork, turkey, or lean lamb)
½ cup tomato paste
Two 14.5-ounce cans diced tomatoes
4 cups chicken stock
4 to 6 garlic cloves, finely chopped
¾ cup roughly chopped flat-leaf parsley
¼ cup grated Parmesan

Green salad

---

372 calories; 33 g protein; 16 g carb; 20 g fat; 2 g saturated fat; 73 mg cholesterol; 5 g fiber; 546 mg sodium

This recipe makes about twice as much bolognese sauce as you need. Store the leftovers in the fridge or freezer and enjoy them on an evening when you don't have time to cook a meal from scratch. If you're serving it with pasta, remember that different pastas have different GI ratings—the thicker the better.

Preheat the oven to 400°F and line a baking sheet with parchment paper.

Slice the tops off the red peppers and remove the membrane and seeds (reserve the tops for later). Put the lids back on, place the peppers on the sheet and bake for 15 minutes. Mop up any liquid that forms in the peppers with paper towels.

Meanwhile, heat the oil in a large nonstick frying pan over medium heat and cook the onion, celery, and carrots for 4 to 5 minutes or until softened, stirring regularly. Remove and set aside. Spray the pan with olive oil, then add the ground chicken and cook for 3 to 4 minutes, stirring constantly, until cooked through. Remove and reserve any liquid that forms to avoid stewing. Return the vegetables to the pan with the chicken, then stir in the tomato paste, diced tomatoes, reserved liquid, and half the stock. Bring to a boil, then reduce the heat and simmer for 30 minutes.

Pour in the remaining stock and cook for another 30 minutes, stirring regularly. Add the garlic and parsley and cook for a further 5 minutes.

Preheat the oven to 400°F. Remove the lids from the peppers and spoon in the chicken bolognese. Cover with parchment paper and bake for 15 minutes. Put the tops on the peppers and return to the oven until they start to blister.

To serve, place the peppers on serving plates, sprinkle with Parmesan, and serve with a green salad.

> For a terrific low-carb meal, stuff large white mushroom caps with the chicken bolognese and top with ricotta. Bake in a preheated 350°F oven for 15 to 20 minutes or until the mushrooms are cooked. Another low-GI variation is to toss the sauce with buttered cabbage (page 144) or serve it over cannellini or butter beans.

≡ Spoon some chicken bolognese on low-GI whole grain toast and top with a little grated mozzarella—great for kids.

☰ Garnish with finely chopped preserved lemon and a little low-fat sour cream or plain yogurt.

< Slow-Cooked Chicken with Artichokes and Cannellini Beans

The luscious combination of green olives, wine, chicken, and artichokes is perfectly complemented by the tart freshness of the gremolata.

Serves 4 | Prep time: 20 minutes | Cooking time: 1 hour

1 tablespoon olive oil
1 onion, cut into 8 wedges through the root end
2 garlic cloves, crushed
1 cup pitted marinated green olives, sliced in half on the
    diagonal or lightly crushed
3 tablespoons white wine
1 cup marinated artichokes, cut into quarters
One 15-ounce can cannellini beans, rinsed and drained
2 cups tomato passata or tomato sauce
1½ cups chicken stock
8 bone-in chicken thighs, skin removed
½ cup roughly chopped flat-leaf parsley
Flaky sea salt and freshly ground black pepper to taste

Green salad

GREMOLATA
2 tablespoons grated lemon zest
1 tablespoon lemon juice
2 garlic cloves, finely chopped
½ cup roughly chopped flat-leaf parsley

Heat the oil in a large Dutch oven over medium-high heat and cook the onion, garlic, and olives for 2 to 3 minutes. Pour in the wine and bring to a boil. Add the artichokes, beans, tomato passata, and stock and return to a boil. Add the chicken and parsley, then reduce the heat and simmer for 50 to 55 minutes, partially covered. To make the gremolata, combine all the ingredients in a small bowl. About 5 minutes before serving, stir in most of the gremolata, reserving a little to garnish. Season with salt and pepper and serve with a green salad.

708 calories; 45 g protein; 40 g carb; 41 g fat; 4 g saturated fat; 143 mg cholesterol; 11 g fiber; 1282 mg sodium

To reduce fat and sodium, use frozen artichokes.

Baked Chicken in Maple, Soy and Sage Marinade

The unique flavor of maple syrup is the secret behind this dish. Always use pure syrup, rather than the cheaper "maple-flavored" version—it really does make a difference.

Serves 4 to 6 | Prep time: 15 minutes | Cooking time: 30 minutes

MAPLE, SOY AND SAGE MARINADE
2 tablespoons lemon juice
3 tablespoons pure maple syrup
2 tablespoons low-sodium tamari or soy sauce
2 tablespoons olive oil
2 tablespoons chopped sage leaves

8 bone-in chicken thighs, skin removed
2 tablespoons sesame seeds, toasted
8 ounces sugar snap peas or green beans, topped and tailed
2 ears corn
2 large carrots, cut into batons

Green salad

Preheat the oven to 400°F. Line a large baking sheet with parchment paper.

Place the marinade ingredients in a lidded jar and shake well.

Place the chicken pieces on the baking sheet and brush well with half the marinade. Bake for 15 minutes, basting every 5 minutes or so. Remove from the oven and reduce the temperature to 350°F. Sprinkle the sesame seeds over the chicken, then bake for another 15 minutes.

About 5 minutes before you're ready to serve, lightly steam the peas, corn, and carrots. Cut the kernels off the cobs in long strips, or cut the cobs into wheels.

In a small saucepan, bring the remaining marinade to a boil.

Place the chicken and vegetables on serving plates and drizzle with the warm marinade. Serve with a green salad.

572 calories; 40 g protein; 38 g carb; 31 g fat; 3 g saturated fat; 141 mg cholesterol; 7 g fiber; 454 mg sodium

Use the marinade with chicken ribs or mini drumsticks to make nibbles with drinks or as a healthy protein snack for the kids.

≡ Toss some baby carrots with the onions and serve the chicken on a bed of steamed basmati rice and wheels of corn.

Lemon and Garlic Roast Chicken with Eggplant Wedges

Even if you are not mad about eggplant, you will love this dish—particularly if you like soy and garlic. Garlic features in a lot of my recipes; I love it for its flavor as well as its medicinal properties.

Preheat the oven to 350°F. Lightly salt the eggplant and set aside for 15 minutes, then rinse and drain on paper towels, pressing gently to remove as much liquid as possible. (This process of making the eggplant sweat helps to remove any bitterness—you don't need to do it with young eggplants.)

To make the lemon and garlic marinade, place all the ingredients in a glass jar with a lid and shake well.

Arrange the onion and eggplant segments in the middle of a 9 × 13-inch baking dish or casserole.

Wash the chicken under cold water and pat dry with paper towels. Place breast-side down on the onions and eggplant and pour the marinade over the top. Stuff the reserved lemon halves and half the garlic into the chicken cavity and scatter the remaining garlic cloves around the chicken. Spray the vegetables with oil. Season the chicken with sea salt and bake for 1¼ to 1½ hours, basting every 30 minutes or so.

Remove the chicken and vegetables from the oven. Transfer the chicken to a plate, cover with foil, and let rest for 10 minutes. Place the eggplants and onions in a clean baking dish and return to the oven while the chicken is resting.

Pour the chicken cooking juices from the baking dish into a saucepan, removing as much oil as possible, add the stock, and gently heat. Add the chicken resting juices to the pan, then pour into a pitcher or gravy boat.

To serve, remove and discard the skin from the chicken (if you are watching your fat intake). Cut the chicken into pieces and place on a large serving sheet with the roasted vegetables and lemon wedges around the chicken. Serve with the warmed chicken juices and steamed snow peas.

> Depending on the size of your baking dish, there may be only a small amount of marinade remaining. This is easily fixed—simply drizzle freshly squeezed lemon juice and a little extra soy sauce over the chicken.

SERVES 4 TO 6
Prep time: 20 minutes
Cooking time: 1½ hours

2 medium or 8 baby eggplants, cut in half horizontally and then into wedges
Flaky sea salt
4 large red onions, each cut into 8 segments through the root end
One 4-pound chicken, trimmed of excess fat
8 to 10 garlic cloves, smashed
Olive oil spray
½ cup chicken stock
Lemon wedges
1 pound steamed snow peas, green beans, and/or sugar snaps, topped and tailed

LEMON AND GARLIC MARINADE
¼ cup fresh lemon juice (reserve the spent lemon halves for later)
3 tablespoons low-sodium tamari or soy sauce
4 star anise pods, broken (or 1 teaspoon Chinese five-spice or star anise powder)
2 tablespoons pure maple syrup
8 to 10 garlic cloves, smashed
2 tablespoons olive oil

484 calories; 50 g protein; 43 g carb; 13 g fat; 2 g saturated fat; 137 mg cholesterol; 11 g fiber; 814 mg sodium

Main Meals
with Meat

The traditional concept of "meat and three veg" is embraced in this section and given a substantial shake-up by drawing on different cuisines and using plenty of fresh herbs and spices. The high-protein mains are matched with low-GI vegetables designed to offer nutritiously dense meals that please the eye and satisfy even the fussiest of palates.

Veal and Red Pepper Casserole with Pomegranate Molasses

SERVES 6
Prep time: 25 minutes
Cooking time: 2 hours 20 minutes

1¾ pounds boneless veal leg roast, cut into 1¼-inch dice
Flaky sea salt and freshly ground black pepper to taste
1 tablespoon olive oil
1 onion, cut into wedges
2 carrots, sliced
2 cups chicken stock
2 red bell peppers, cut into 1¼-inch squares
One 14.5-ounce can crushed tomatoes
2 tablespoons pomegranate molasses
¼ cup tomato paste
2 garlic cloves, finely chopped
¾ cup finely chopped flat-leaf parsley, plus extra to garnish
12 ounces farfalle pasta
8 ounces snow peas, topped and tailed
8 ounces shelled peas

512 calories; 42 g protein; 64 g carb; 9 g fat; 1 g saturated fat; 171 mg cholesterol; 7 g fiber; 485 mg sodium

Pomegranate molasses is a concentrated liquid commonly used in Middle Eastern cooking, adding a tartness and astringency to both sweet and savory dishes. Once you have a bottle in your pantry, you'll find yourself experimenting with it again and again.

Season the veal with salt and pepper. Heat the oil in a heavy-bottomed ovenproof casserole dish over medium heat and cook the veal for 2 to 3 minutes or until lightly golden. Remove and drain on paper towels.

Add the onion and carrots to the pan and cook for 2 to 3 minutes until softened (add a little stock if necessary). Add the red peppers and return the veal to the dish, then stir in the crushed tomatoes, remaining stock, pomegranate molasses, and tomato paste. Increase the heat and bring to a boil, then reduce the heat to medium-high and cook for 10 minutes. Reduce the heat to medium and simmer, covered, for 1 hour. Remove the lid and simmer for 30 minutes. Stir in the garlic and parsley and simmer for another 30 minutes. Just before serving, garnish with extra parsley.

Meanwhile, cook the farfalle according to the package instructions. Drain.

About 5 minutes prior to serving, cover the snow peas with boiling water and allow to sit for 3 to 4 minutes. Drain. Boil or steam the shelled peas until cooked to your liking. Mix with the snow peas.

Divide the farfalle among soup bowls and spoon the veal casserole over the top. Serve with the mixed peas.

Leave out the pasta if you like and serve the casserole on a bed of fresh or cooked baby spinach (very low carb) or steamed basmati rice. Alternatively, add some cubed sweet potato or a can of drained and rinsed beans for some extra low-GI carbs.

≡ If you like, this dish can be made with lamb loin chops instead of the veal.

Veal Scaloppine with Lemon Parsley Crumbs

Serves 4 | Prep time: 15 minutes, plus soaking time | Cooking time: 15 minutes

1½ pounds veal scallopine, cut into 3-ounce pieces (don't pound the meat)
1 cup low-fat milk
Flaky sea salt and freshly ground black pepper to taste
Olive oil spray
1½ tablespoons butter
12 ounces baby green beans, topped not tailed
3 tablespoons chicken stock
1 tablespoon lemon juice
1 tablespoon low-fat plain yogurt

Green salad

LEMON PARSLEY CRUMBS
¼ cup ground, slivered, or crushed almonds
½ cup finely chopped flat-leaf parsley
2 tablespoons grated lemon zest
2 garlic cloves, finely chopped
Olive oil spray

Soak the veal in the milk for at least an hour prior to cooking (or overnight if possible). This will tenderize the meat.

For the lemon parsley crumbs, combine the almonds, parsley, lemon zest, and garlic. Heat a large nonstick frying pan over medium heat and spray well with oil. Add the mixture and cook for 3 to 4 minutes or until the almonds turn golden. Transfer to a bowl and season with salt and pepper.

Remove the veal from the milk and pat dry with paper towels. Season with salt and pepper. Wipe out the pan and place over medium-high heat, then spray with olive oil and add the butter. When sizzling, add the veal pieces and cook for 1 to 2 minutes on each side, depending on the thickness of the veal. Remove and keep warm.

Steam the green beans until just tender.

Meanwhile, return the frying pan to medium-high heat and add the stock and lemon juice. Bring to a boil, then remove from the heat and stir in the yogurt.

Place the veal and the green beans on serving plates. Stir the veal resting juices into the yogurt sauce. Drizzle the veal and beans with sauce, and sprinkle the veal with lemon parsley crumbs. Serve with a green salad.

474 calories; 41 g protein; 14 g carb; 29 g fat; 4 g saturated fat; 140 mg cholesterol; 6 g fiber; 366 mg sodium

Veal Scaloppine in Tomato and Basil Sauce with Fresh Ricotta

For this recipe, it's worth seeking out the best ricotta you can buy, with no added stabilizers or preservatives.

Serves 4 | Prep time: 15 minutes, plus soaking time | Cooking time: 25 minutes

1½ pounds veal scallopine, cut into 3-ounce pieces (don't pound the meat)
1 cup low-fat milk
3 cups tomato sauce or tomato passata
4 garlic cloves, finely chopped
2 tablespoons tomato paste
½ cup roughly chopped basil or flat-leaf parsley, plus extra to garnish
Flaky sea salt and freshly ground black pepper to taste
Olive oil spray
1½ tablespoons butter
½ cup fresh low-fat ricotta
3 tablespoons shredded Parmesan

Green salad

Soak the veal in the milk for at least an hour prior to cooking (or overnight if possible). This will tenderize the meat.

Preheat the oven to 350°F.

Combine the tomato sauce, garlic, tomato paste, and basil in a medium saucepan and cook over medium-high heat for 10 minutes.

Remove the veal from the milk and pat dry with paper towels. Season with salt and pepper. Heat a nonstick grill or frying pan over medium heat, spray with olive oil, and add the butter. When sizzling, add the veal and cook for 1 to 2 minutes on each side, depending on the thickness.

Spoon a little tomato sauce into an ovenproof dish large enough to hold the veal in a single layer. Arrange the veal pieces over the sauce, then ladle on the remaining sauce. Place some ricotta over each piece of veal and sprinkle with Parmesan. Lightly spray with olive oil and bake for about 10 minutes until the Parmesan has melted. Garnish with a few extra basil leaves and serve with a green salad.

489 calories; 46 g protein; 25 g carb; 24 g fat; 5 g saturated fat; 148 mg cholesterol; 5 g fiber; 442 mg sodium

≡ If you want a golden finish, pop the dish under the broiler for a few minutes.

≡ For an inexpensive alternative, use loin chops instead of the rib chops.

< Lamb Rib Chops in Maple and Red Wine Vinegar Marinade

These small chops, sometimes called lollipop chops, are also delicious cooked on the grill—serve them as finger food with drinks.

Serves 4 | Prep time: 10 minutes, plus marinating time | Cooking time: 10 minutes

MAPLE AND RED WINE VINEGAR MARINADE
2 tablespoons pure maple syrup
2 tablespoons extra virgin olive oil
2 tablespoons low-sodium tamari or soy sauce
2 tablespoons red wine vinegar (or apple cider vinegar or lemon juice)

1¾ pounds lamb rib chops
Olive oil spray
3 tablespoons chicken stock
12 ounces broccolini or broccoli
Sweet potato chips (page 146)

To make the marinade, place all the ingredients in a glass jar with a lid and shake well. Place the lamb in a nonmetallic dish, add the marinade, and turn to coat. Cover and leave for at least 30 minutes (or overnight if time permits).

Heat a large nonstick grill or frying pan over medium-high heat. When hot, spray with oil, then add the lamb and cook for 2 minutes on each side. Remove and cover with foil and then a tea towel, and set aside to rest.

Return the pan to the heat, add the stock and remaining marinade, and bring gently to a simmer. Cook for 4 to 5 minutes until the sauce has reduced slightly.

Meanwhile, steam the broccolini.

To serve, arrange the sweet potato discs on four plates. Stack the lamb cutlets on top of each other and drizzle with the sauce. Place the broccolini on the side.

618 calories; 41 g protein; 24 g carb; 40 g fat; 14 g saturated fat; 132 mg cholesterol; 5 g fiber; 439 mg sodium

The cutlets may also be served with Broccoli with Lemon Olive Oil and Parmesan (page 143). Add rosemary sprigs, a little preserved lemon, or grated lemon zest for extra zing.

Veal and Sage Roast with Spinach and Cannellini Beans

Like all lean cuts of meat, veal leg can dry out if overcooked, so it is important to let it rest for a while after baking. If you do this, the meat will be tender and juicy.

Serves 4 | Prep time: 15 minutes | Cooking time: 1¼ hours

2 pounds veal leg round
Flaky sea salt and freshly ground black pepper to taste
2 tablespoons finely chopped sage leaves
1 tablespoon olive oil
1 cup chicken or veal stock
2 red onions, each cut into 8 wedges through the root end
½ cup white wine or verjuice
One 15-ounce can cannellini beans, rinsed and drained
1 teaspoon Dijon mustard
2 tablespoons low-fat sour cream or low-fat cream cheese
9 cups baby spinach

Preheat the oven to 350°F.

Season the veal with salt and pepper and sprinkle with half the sage. Heat the oil in a large Dutch oven over medium-high heat and cook the veal for 3 minutes. Turn and cook until golden on all sides, then remove the veal and set aside.

Add a little stock or water to the pot and cook the onions until softened. Return the veal to the pot, then pour in the wine and simmer until the liquid has reduced slightly. Add the remaining stock, then cover and bake for 45 minutes. Stir in the beans and bake for another 15 minutes for medium-rare veal, or longer if preferred. Remove the pot from the oven and set aside for 10 minutes, then take out the veal and cut into slices.

Place the pot over low heat and simmer for 1 to 2 minutes. Stir in the mustard and sour cream and season with salt and pepper.

To serve, divide the spinach and veal slices among four plates and spoon the beans and sauce over the top.

496 calories; 61 g protein; 27 g carb; 14 g fat; 4 g saturated fat; 199 mg cholesterol; 8 g fiber; 552 mg sodium

≡ If there is not enough liquid to make a sauce, add a little stock and a dash of white wine.

Roast Leg of Lamb with Oregano, Olives and Lemon

A tasty dish for all seasons and great if you're feeding a crowd. During the summer months, I usually serve it with a simple salad of baby spinach, vine-ripened tomato, cucumber, feta, and finely sliced red onion.

Place the lemon zest, lemon juice, salt, pepper, oregano, and oil in a glass jar with a lid and shake well. Massage well into the lamb, then set aside to marinate for at least an hour out of the fridge (or overnight in the fridge, if time permits).

Preheat the oven to 400°F and line a large roasting pan with parchment paper.

Place the onions, garlic, and olives in the center of the sheet and position the lamb on top. Bake for 30 minutes. Reduce the temperature to 350°F and bake for another 30 minutes for medium-rare, or to taste (cover the lamb with foil if the oregano starts to blacken). Remove the lamb, cover with foil and then a tea towel, and leave to rest for at least 20 minutes. Reduce the oven temperature to 325°F.

Transfer the onion, garlic, and olives to a small ovenproof dish, cover with foil, and return to the oven. Pour the juices from the pan into a small saucepan, add any lamb resting juices, and bring to a gentle simmer. Pour into a pitcher or gravy boat.

Meanwhile, steam the peas, then drizzle with a little lemon olive oil and season with salt to taste.

Carve the lamb into slices. Divide the mash among six plates and place the lamb on top, followed by the onion, garlic, and olives. Place the steamed peas on the side and take the warmed juices to the table. Serve with a dollop of tzatziki.

Kid Friendly This seems to appeal to most kids (although some may pick out the olives!). My kids prefer the mash to be made just with sweet potato, without the celeriac, and I often stir a little mint and goat cheese or feta into the peas.

SERVES 6
Prep time: 20 minutes, plus
    marinating time
Cooking time: 1 hour

Grated zest of 2 lemons
2 tablespoons lemon juice
1 teaspoon flaky sea salt, plus extra
    for seasoning
1 teaspoon freshly ground black
    pepper
2 tablespoons dried oregano
2 tablespoons olive oil
One 3-pound boned leg of lamb,
    trimmed of excess fat
4 red onions, cut into quarters
    through the root end
10 garlic cloves, crushed with the
    side of a knife
1 cup marinated kalamata olives,
    pitted and halved
18 ounces sugar snap peas or snow
    peas, topped and tailed
Lemon olive oil, for drizzling
Celeriac and Roasted Sweet Potato
    Mash (page 146)
½ cup low-fat tzatziki (page 15)

719 calories; 53 g protein; 70 g carb;
25 g fat; 6 g saturated fat; 157 mg
cholesterol; 12 g fiber; 1016 mg sodium

Slow-Cooked Lamb with Tomato, Garlic and Parsley

As with most slow-cooked soups and stews, this tastes even better the next day. Add a little grated lemon or orange zest to the garlic and parsley topping for an extra level of flavor.

Serves 4 | Prep time: 20 minutes | Cooking time: 2½ hours

One 2-pound lamb shoulder, cut into large pieces (or use forequarter chops, trimmed of excess fat)
Flaky sea salt and freshly ground black pepper to taste
1 tablespoon olive oil
1 onion, cut into 8 wedges through the root end
2 carrots, sliced
2 red bell peppers, cut into 1-inch squares
2 cups chicken or beef stock
½ cup red wine
3 cups tomato passata or tomato sauce
½ cup tomato paste
2 rosemary sprigs, plus extra leaves to garnish
1 cup roughly chopped flat-leaf parsley
4 garlic cloves, finely chopped
Cauliflower and White Bean Puree (page 148)

Season the lamb with salt and pepper. Heat the oil in a large Dutch oven over medium-high heat and cook the lamb for 2 minutes on each side. Drain on paper towels.

Add the onion, carrots, and red peppers to the pot and cook for 5 minutes, stirring occasionally (add a little stock if the vegetables begin to stick). Pour in the wine and bring to a boil for 1 minute. Return the lamb to the pot and add the tomato passata, tomato paste, remaining stock, rosemary, and half the parsley and garlic. Simmer, partially covered, over low heat for 2 to 2½ hours (or bake in a 350°F oven, if preferred).

To serve, spoon the cauliflower puree onto four plates and ladle the lamb and vegetables over the top. Sprinkle with the extra rosemary and the remaining garlic and parsley.

---

703 calories; 66 g protein; 63 g carb; 21 g fat; 6 g saturated fat; 170 mg cholesterol; 18 g fiber; 857 mg sodium

Kid Friendly Serve over farfalle pasta or on low-GI toast.

Lemon Pepper Lamb with Braised Eggplant >

Serves 4 | Prep time: 20 minutes, plus standing time | Cooking time: 20 minutes

1 teaspoon flaky sea salt, plus extra for sprinkling
1 teaspoon freshly ground black pepper
¼ cup grated lemon zest
1¾ pounds lamb loin
6 small or 2 medium eggplants, cut into 1-inch cubes
Olive oil spray
2 red onions, each cut into 8 wedges through the root end
1 cup chicken stock
1 cup canned chickpeas, rinsed and drained
½ cup roughly chopped flat-leaf parsley
2 garlic cloves, finely chopped
2 tablespoons lemon juice
1 tablespoon olive oil
2 teaspoons balsamic vinegar
6 cups baby spinach
½ cup low-fat tzatziki (page 15)

Combine the salt, pepper, and 2 tablespoons lemon zest and press well into the lamb. Set aside.

Lightly salt the eggplant and set aside for 15 minutes, then rinse and drain on paper towels.

Heat a large nonstick frying pan over medium-high heat. Spray well with oil and cook the onions until softened. Lightly spray the eggplant with oil. Add to the pan and cook for 4 to 5 minutes, shaking the pan regularly (add a little stock if it starts to stick). Add the chickpeas and remaining stock and cook, covered, for another 5 minutes. Stir in the parsley, garlic, remaining lemon zest, and 1 tablespoon lemon juice.

Meanwhile, heat a nonstick grill pan over medium-high heat. Spray with oil and cook the lamb for 2 to 3 minutes on each side for medium-rare, or longer if preferred. Remove the lamb, cover with foil and then a tea towel, and leave to rest for 5 minutes. Cut into ¾-inch-thick slices.

While the meat is resting, combine the olive oil, balsamic vinegar, and remaining lemon juice in a small saucepan and gently warm through. Add any lamb resting juices.

Divide the spinach, lamb, and eggplant mixture among four plates. Drizzle with the dressing and serve with tzatziki.

---

555 calories; 51 g protein; 39 g carb; 22 g fat; 7 g saturated fat; 149 mg cholesterol; 13 g fiber; 828 mg sodium

Mild Curried Lamb in Coconut Milk with Green Beans and Yogurt

I've kept this curry deliberately mild so it is suitable for the whole family. To spice it up, simply add more curry powder or dried chile flakes, or serve with mango or lime chutney (keep an eye on the sugar content).

Preheat the oven to 325°F.

Season the lamb with a little salt. Heat the oil in a Dutch oven over high heat and cook the lamb for about 30 seconds each side. Remove and drain on paper towels.

Add the onion, carrots, and a little stock and cook for a few minutes until the onion has softened. Stir in the curry powder, ginger, and garam masala and cook for 1 minute. Slowly add the coconut milk, remaining stock, and cinnamon sticks, stirring constantly. Return the lamb to the pot, then cover and bake for 1 to 1½ hours. Add the turnips after 30 minutes of cooking.

Meanwhile, steam the beans until tender.

To serve, ladle the lamb mixture into bowls and garnish with mint leaves. Place the beans on the side, dollop with a spoonful of yogurt, and serve with steamed rice.

Kid Friendly The turnips are sweet and often mistaken by young palates for potatoes, but if turnips are not your thing, use small cubes of sweet potato instead—they're higher in carbs but still nutritious, delicious, and low GI.

SERVES 4
Prep time: 20 minutes
Cooking time: 2 hours

One 1½ pound lamb shoulder, cut into large pieces
Flaky sea salt
1 tablespoon olive oil
1 onion, finely chopped
2 carrots, sliced
1 cup chicken stock
1 teaspoon curry powder
1 teaspoon ground ginger or 1 tablespoon grated ginger
1 teaspoon garam masala
1 cup light coconut milk
2 cinnamon sticks, broken in half
12 baby turnips, scrubbed and trimmed, leaving ½-inch green tops
12 ounces baby green beans, topped not tailed
Mint leaves, torn
¼ cup low-fat plain yogurt
2 cups steamed basmati rice

752 calories; 43 g protein; 57 g carb; 46 g fat; 20 g saturated fat; 142 mg cholesterol; 8 g fiber; 423 mg sodium

High Protein, Low GI, Bold Flavor

Roast Pork in Cinnamon and Soy with Peas and Bok Choy

This is also delicious served with mashed sweet potatoes, wilted spinach, steamed basmati rice, or steamed broccoli.

Serves 4 | Prep time: 20 minutes | Cooking time: 35 minutes

1¾ pounds pork tenderloin or two 14-ounce fillets
Olive oil spray
½ cup chicken stock
1 pound sugar snap peas and/or snow peas, topped not tailed
2 bunches bok choy, cut in half lengthwise

CINNAMON AND SOY MARINADE
3 tablespoons low-sodium tamari or soy sauce
3 tablespoons rice wine vinegar
2 teaspoons sesame oil
1 tablespoon mushroom soy sauce, optional
1 tablespoon pure maple syrup
1 teaspoon Chinese five-spice powder
2 cinnamon sticks, broken in half
4 star anise pods, optional

Preheat the oven to 350°F.

Place all the marinade ingredients in a glass jar with a lid and shake well. Pour half the marinade over the pork and massage in well. Pat dry with paper towels just before cooking.

Heat a nonstick frying pan over medium-high heat, spray with oil, and cook the pork for 2 to 3 minutes on each side. Transfer the pork to a baking dish and spray with a little more oil. Bake for 25 to 30 minutes. Remove the pork, cover with foil and then a tea towel, and leave to rest for 10 minutes before slicing.

Meanwhile, pour the remaining marinade into a small saucepan. Add the stock and any resting juices and bring to a gentle simmer.

Steam the peas and bok choy until tender.

Divide the bok choy among four plates. Arrange the pork slices over the bok choy and ladle the warm sauce over the top. Serve with the peas.

397 calories; 53 g protein; 25 g carb; 10 g fat; 2 g saturated fat; 131 mg cholesterol; 9 g fiber; 792 mg sodium

Slow-Cooked Pork with Fennel and Sage

This dish is deceptively creamy, but it can be enjoyed guilt-free. Enjoy it over low-GI cannellini beans or noodles.

Serves 6 | Prep time: 20 minutes | Cooking time: 3 hours

2½-pound pork neck, trimmed of fat
Flaky sea salt and freshly ground black pepper to taste
1 tablespoon olive oil
Olive oil spray
2 large fennel bulbs, each cut into 8 wedges
2 cups chicken stock
½ cup white wine or verjuice
2 cups skim milk
2 cups whole milk
8 garlic cloves, smashed
¼ cup sage leaves
12 ounces green beans, topped not tailed
9 cups baby spinach

GREMOLATA
2 tablespoons grated lemon zest
1 tablespoon lemon juice
2 garlic cloves, finely chopped
½ cup roughly chopped flat-leaf parsley

Season the pork with salt and pepper. Heat the oil in a large Dutch oven over medium-high heat and cook the pork for 2 to 3 minutes on each side. Remove and drain on paper towels.

Spray the pot with oil then add the fennel and cook for 4 to 5 minutes or until it starts to turn golden brown (add a little stock if it starts to stick). Add the wine and bring to a boil. Cook for another 2 to 3 minutes, then add the skim milk, whole milk, remaining stock, garlic, and sage and bring to a simmer. Return the pork to the pot, then reduce the heat and simmer, covered, for 2½ to 3 hours.

Meanwhile, combine all the gremolata ingredients in a small bowl. Steam the green beans until just tender.

Remove the pork from the pot and cut into thick slices. Return the slices to the pot and stir in the gremolata.

To serve, place a handful of spinach in each bowl, then spoon the pork, vegetables, and sauce over the top.

621 calories; 74 g protein; 24 g carb; 23 g fat; 8 g saturated fat; 193 mg cholesterol; 7 g fiber; 534 mg sodium

Pork Chops with Apples and Balsamic Vinegar

SERVES 4

Prep time: 15 minutes,
    plus marinating time
Cooking time: 20 minutes

APPLE AND BALSAMIC MARINADE

3 tablespoons olive oil

2 tablespoons apple juice concentrate

3 tablespoons aged balsamic vinegar

1 teaspoon sambal oelek

Four 7-ounce pork cutlets or midloin
    pork chops

Olive oil spray

2 apples, sliced with skin on

½ to ¾ cup chicken stock

12 ounces green beans, topped not
    tailed (or use asparagus)

12 ounces baby carrots, washed and
    trimmed

Buttered Cabbage (page 144)

692 calories; 46 g protein; 36 g carb; 42 g fat; 12 g saturated fat; 149 mg cholesterol; 11 g fiber; 449 mg sodium

This is a lovely combination—the sweetness of the apples and delicate flavor of the pork and cabbage are a great marriage. Serve it with high-protein quinoa for a heartier, high-protein meal.

Place all the marinade ingredients in a glass jar with a lid and shake well. Pour the marinade over the pork and leave to marinate for at least 30 minutes (overnight if time permits). Remove the pork, reserving the marinade.

Heat a medium heavy-bottomed frying pan or grill pan over medium-high heat. When hot, spray with oil, then reduce the heat to medium and cook the pork for 4 minutes on each side, or longer to taste. Remove the pork, cover with foil, and set aside to rest for about 10 minutes.

Meanwhile, spray another frying pan with a little oil, add the sliced apples, and cook for 2 to 3 minutes over medium-high heat. Add ½ cup stock and cook over medium heat for 4 to 5 minutes, stirring regularly. Pour in the remaining stock if the apples start to dry out. Add the remaining marinade and pork resting juices and simmer gently until the liquid has reduced slightly.

Steam the beans and carrots until just tender.

To serve, spoon the buttered cabbage onto four plates and place the pork on top. Ladle the apple and sauce over the pork and stack the beans and carrots on the side.

During the warmer months, serve the pork chops with a simple salad of finely sliced red cabbage, red apple, and carrot, dressed with plain yogurt, lemon juice, salt, and pepper.

≡ For a quick and colorful alternative, serve the chops with red sauerkraut instead of buttered cabbage.

Sizzling Beef with Ginger and Soy

Good-quality beef tenderloin needs minimal embellishment. Here it is infused with the flavors of soy, garlic, and ginger and quickly stir-fried until tender. Serve this dish over steamed rice.

Serves 4 | Prep time: 20 minutes, plus marinating time | Cooking time: 15 minutes

1 cup bean sprouts
One 1½-pound beef tenderloin, cut into ¼- to ½-inch-thick slices
1 to 2 tablespoons olive oil
2 carrots, cut into matchsticks
8 ounces snow peas, topped not tailed
2 cups steamed basmati rice, optional

SOY AND GINGER MARINADE
½ cup low-sodium tamari or soy sauce
3 garlic cloves, crushed
1 small onion, finely chopped
2 tablespoons grated ginger
1 tablespoon olive oil

Soak the bean sprouts in cold water for about 10 minutes.

Place all the marinade ingredients and ¼ cup water in a glass jar with a lid and shake well. Combine the meat and marinade in a nonmetallic dish and leave to marinate for at least 15 minutes (overnight if time permits).

Heat 1 tablespoon oil in a wok or large nonstick frying pan over high heat. Working in small batches so the meat doesn't stew, shake off the marinade from the beef slices (reserving it), and add the slices to the wok. Sear each side for about 10 seconds, then remove and drain on paper towels.

Wipe out the wok and return it to medium-high heat. Add a little oil and cook the carrots for 2 to 3 minutes, adding a dash of water to prevent sticking, then cover and steam for a minute or two. Add the snow peas and drained bean sprouts, shake vigorously, and cook for 1 to 2 more minutes.

Meanwhile, pour the marinade into a small saucepan and simmer gently for a few minutes.

Divide the meat and vegetables among four plates and drizzle the hot marinade over the top.

700 calories; 41 g protein; 49 g carb; 44 g fat; 15 g saturated fat; 119 mg cholesterol; 4 g fiber; 1187 mg sodium

Chinese Five-Spice Pork > with Roasted Pears

Roasting the shallots and pears intensifies the flavors, giving a sweet, mellow flavor base to this dish.

Serves 4 | Prep time: 15 minutes | Cooking time: 45 minutes

12 shallots, peeled
2 firm bosc pears, cut into wedges
Olive oil spray
Flaky sea salt to taste
1 tablespoon Chinese five-spice powder
One 1¾-pound pork fillet or tenderloin
1 pound choy sum, cut into wedges
2 ears corn, kernels cut from cob
1 tablespoon oyster sauce or hoisin sauce
2 teaspoons butter
1 tablespoon low-sodium tamari or soy sauce
3 tablespoons chicken stock
2 cups steamed basmati rice

Preheat the oven to 400°F and line a large roasting pan with parchment paper. Spread the shallots and pear wedges in the pan, spray with oil, and sprinkle with salt. Bake for 15 minutes.

Meanwhile, rub the Chinese five-spice powder and some sea salt over the pork. Heat a large nonstick frying pan over medium heat, spray with oil and cook the pork for 3 minutes on each side or until golden.

Add the pork to the pan with the shallots and pears and reduce the oven temperature to 350°F. Bake the pork, shallots, and pears for another 20 to 25 minutes. Remove the pork, cover, and allow to rest for 10 minutes. Return the shallots and pears to the oven.

Meanwhile, steam the choy sum and corn for 3 to 4 minutes or until wilted. Warm the oyster sauce and butter in a medium saucepan over medium heat, then add the choy sum and corn and toss to coat.

Place the frying pan used to brown the pork over medium-high heat. Add the soy sauce, stock, and any resting juices from the meat and warm through.

Cut the pork into thick slices. Place a little rice on each plate and arrange the pork slices on top, followed by the shallots and pear wedges. Drizzle with the sauce and serve with the vegetables.

507 calories; 49 g protein; 62 g carb; 14 g fat; 5 g saturated fat; 137 mg cholesterol; 4 g fiber; 467 mg sodium

≡ If you like, place the pork slices directly in the warm sauce and toss before serving.

Beef Sirloin and Roasted Jerusalem Artichokes with Mustard Cream

SERVES 6
Prep time: 15 minutes
Cooking time: 45 minutes

One 2½-pound beef sirloin
Olive oil, for brushing
Flaky sea salt and freshly ground
    black pepper to taste
3 large onions, each cut into 8 wedges
    through the root end
6 garlic cloves, smashed
Olive oil spray
20 Jerusalem artichokes (about 1
    pound), well scrubbed and trimmed
8 sprigs rosemary or oregano
1¼ pounds asparagus, trimmed

MUSTARD CREAM
1 garlic clove, finely chopped
1 tablespoon olive oil
3 tablespoons low-fat sour cream
1 teaspoon grainy mustard
Pinch of flaky sea salt

---

579 calories; 41 g protein; 26 g carb; 34 g
fat; 13 g saturated fat; 130 mg cholesterol;
5 g fiber; 279 mg sodium

When buying Jerusalem artichokes, look for young tubers as they have a crisp white flesh and deliciously nutty flavor. They're wonderful with beef and lamb, roasted sweet potatoes, and carrots.

Remove the beef from the fridge at least 1 hour prior to cooking so it comes to room temperature (this will ensure even cooking). Preheat the oven to 425°F and line a large roasting pan with parchment paper.

Brush the meat with oil and season with salt and pepper. Place the onions and garlic in the pan and spray with oil. Position the meat over most of the onions and scatter the Jerusalem artichokes and rosemary sprigs around the pan. Spray with oil and sprinkle with salt. Bake for 30 minutes for medium-rare or longer to taste. Remove the meat from the pan, cover with foil and then a tea towel, and leave to rest for at least 20 minutes.

Reduce the oven temperature to 350°F. Return the vegetables to the oven and bake for another 10 minutes.

Meanwhile, steam the asparagus.

To make the mustard cream, place all the ingredients in a small bowl and mix well.

Slice the beef and place on a warm platter. Arrange the vegetables around the meat and serve with the mustard cream on the side.

Serve with any of the vegetable mashes in the Sides chapter or with Broccoli with Lemon Olive Oil and Parmesan (page 143). Also try cannellini beans, wilted spinach, or sauerkraut.

Beef and Almond Balls in Homemade Tomato Sauce with Mozzarella

This is a great recipe for feeding large numbers of hungry children, particularly served over quinoa or large rigatoni noodles, topped with fresh ricotta or Parmesan—simple and delicious!

Serves 6 | Prep time: 25 minutes | Cooking time: 1 hour

1 tablespoon olive oil
1 onion, finely chopped
Two 14.5-ounce cans diced tomatoes
2 cups tomato passata or tomato sauce
⅓ cup tomato paste
4 cups chicken stock
Flaky sea salt
½ cup finely chopped flat-leaf parsley
6 garlic cloves, finely chopped
1 cup grated mozzarella

BEEF AND ALMOND BALLS
2 large eggs, lightly beaten
1 pound lean ground beef
1 zucchini, grated or shredded
1 carrot, grated or shredded
3 tablespoons ground almonds
¼ cup tomato paste
1 tablespoon skim milk

Heat the oil in a large heavy-bottomed saucepan over medium-high heat and cook the onion for 2 minutes or until it has softened but not browned. Add the diced tomatoes and their juice, passata, tomato paste, stock, and a good pinch of salt. Bring to a boil, then reduce the heat and simmer for 30 minutes. Stir in the parsley and garlic and simmer for another 20 to 30 minutes.

Meanwhile, to make the beef and almond balls, mix together all the ingredients until well combined. Roll the mixture into walnut-sized balls.

Gently submerge the meatballs in the simmering sauce. You may find the liquid will not totally cover all of the meatballs. This is fine; simply ladle liquid over the exposed meatballs. Gently rotate them after about 5 minutes. Ladle the meatballs and sauce into soup bowls and sprinkle with the mozzarella.

411 calories; 27 g protein; 27 g carb; 23 g fat; 8 g saturated fat; 136 mg cholesterol; 7 g fiber; 434 mg sodium

T-Bone Steak with Parsley and Sour Cream Sauce

You'll find this meal is so quick to throw together, but it packs a real flavor punch. The steak is also delicious served with salad and your favorite mashed vegetable. The accompanying mushroom and spinach recipe will make more than you need here; leftovers taste great warmed and spread on low-GI toast.

Serves 2 | Prep time: 15 minutes | Cooking time: 10 minutes

1 thick T-bone steak (about 1 pound) or 2 pieces of sirloin
Olive oil, for brushing
Flaky sea salt and freshly ground black pepper to taste
Olive oil spray
12 to 14 cherry tomatoes
Sauteed Mushrooms and Spinach (page 152)

PARSLEY AND SOUR CREAM SAUCE
1 teaspoon olive oil
1 garlic clove, finely chopped
1 tablespoon verjuice or white wine
3 tablespoons chicken stock
1 teaspoon Dijon mustard
1 teaspoon low-sodium tamari or soy sauce
1 tablespoon low-fat sour cream
2 tablespoons finely chopped flat-leaf parsley

Remove all visible fat from the steak, then lightly brush with oil and season with salt and pepper. Heat a large nonstick grill pan or frying pan over high heat. When hot, brush with oil and cook the steak for 2 to 3 minutes on each side or until cooked to your liking. Remove the steak, cover with foil and then a tea towel, and leave to rest for a few minutes.

Wipe out the pan and return to medium-high heat. When hot, spray well with olive oil and cook the tomatoes for 4 to 5 minutes, tossing regularly.

To make the sauce, combine the oil, garlic, verjuice, stock, mustard, and tamari in a glass jar with a lid and shake well. Pour into a small saucepan over medium heat and bring just to a boil. Remove from the heat, then stir in the sour cream, parsley, and any steak resting juices.

To serve, cut the steak into two portions (if using a T-bone), drizzle with the sauce, and serve with the cherry tomatoes and Sauteed Mushrooms and Spinach.

699 calories; 51 g protein; 20 g carb; 47 g fat; 14 g saturated fat; 132 mg cholesterol; 6 g fiber; 627 mg sodium

Open Steak Sandwich with Caramelized Onions and Goat Cheese

The recipe for caramelized onions makes about 3 cups—far more than you need here, but it's such a handy thing to have in the fridge. You'll find yourself adding it to sandwiches, soups, and frittatas or just enjoying it with cold meat or chicken and salad.

Steam the beet for 8 to 10 minutes or until just tender. Place in cold water to stop the cooking. When cool enough to handle, remove the skin and shred or slice. (I recommend using kitchen gloves for this or you will end up with bright red fingers!)

Season the steaks with pepper. Heat a large nonstick grill pan or frying pan over high heat. When hot, brush with oil and cook the steaks for 1 minute on each side. Remove from the pan and sprinkle with salt.

To serve, spread a little goat cheese over the toast slices and place the lettuce on top, followed by the steaks. Finish with a layer of beets and caramelized onions, then crumble the remaining cheese over the top. Serve with a knife and fork!

SERVES 4
Prep time: 10 minutes
Cooking time: 15 minutes

1 large beet
Four 4-ounce minute steaks
Flaky sea salt and freshly ground
    black pepper to taste
Olive oil, for brushing
¼ cup soft goat cheese or feta
    marinated in olive oil
4 slices low-GI whole grain bread,
    toasted
3 cups iceberg lettuce or baby
    spinach
¼ cup caramelized onions (see box)

354 calories; 30 g protein; 25 g carb;
16 g fat; 6 g saturated fat; 71 mg
cholesterol; 5 g fiber; 449 mg sodium

To make the caramelized onions, heat ¼ cup olive oil, 3 tablespoons butter, and 2 tablespoons maple syrup in a large Dutch oven over medium heat. When melted, add 12 finely sliced red onions (hint: Use a food processor!) and 2 tablespoons balsamic vinegar and stir well. Reduce the heat and cook gently for 40 to 45 minutes, stirring regularly. If the onions start to stick, add a little chicken stock. Cool and store in the fridge. If you don't have time to make the caramelized onions, just use thinly sliced red onions.

For a lower-carb option, leave out the bread and increase the quantities of beets and spinach for a delicious salad.

Sides

An attractive side dish can transform the simplest of meals into something exceptional. It's easy to experiment with these recipes, and I encourage you to do so. For best results, visit your local farmers' market and see what looks fresh and inviting on the day—it's surprising how little embellishment seasonal produce needs to shine.

< Shredded Cabbage, Dill and Basil

Cabbage is very high in vitamin A and is one of the richest sources of vitamin C. Eating it raw is one of the best ways to reap the nutritional benefits of this powerhouse food.

Serves 6 | Prep time: 15 minutes

½ head savoy cabbage, shredded
1 cup chopped dill
1 cup chopped basil
1 cup chopped flat-leaf parsley
¼ cup soft goat cheese or feta marinated in olive oil
Flaky sea salt and freshly ground black pepper to taste
Vinaigrette (page 138)

Combine all the ingredients in a bowl and toss well. Serve with barbecued meats, chicken, or seafood.

123 calories; 3 g protein; 4 g carb; 12 g fat; 1 g saturated fat; 4 mg cholesterol; 2 g fiber; 54 mg sodium

Use a mandoline to shred the cabbage—it will save time and result in beautifully fine slices.

Eggplant and Pine Nut Tabbouleh

To convert this into a complete meal, add a can of tuna or some shredded leftover lamb or chicken to the salad and dollop with low-fat tzatziki.

Serves 6 to 8 | Prep time: 20 minutes, plus soaking time |
  Cooking time: 40 minutes

½ cup fine or medium bulgur
2 cups chicken stock
1¼ pounds eggplant, cut into bite-sized cubes
Table salt, for sprinkling
Olive oil spray
¼ cup pine nuts or any combination of sesame, pumpkin, or sunflower seeds
3 tablespoons dried currants or freshly chopped dried figs
2 to 3 tablespoons fresh orange juice
4 scallions, finely sliced
1½ cups roughly chopped flat-leaf parsley
¾ cup roughly chopped mint
Grated zest of 1 large orange

Soak the bulgur in the stock for 20 to 30 minutes, depending on the size of the bulgur. Press it in a fine strainer to remove the excess liquid.

Meanwhile, preheat the oven to 400°F and line a large baking sheet with parchment paper.

Lightly salt the eggplant and set aside for 15 minutes, then rinse and drain on paper towels, pressing gently to remove as much liquid as possible. Place the eggplant on the baking sheet in a single layer and spray with oil. Bake for 20 to 25 minutes or until golden, then leave to cool.

Spread out the pine nuts on a baking sheet and bake for 10 minutes or until golden.

Soak the currants in the orange juice.

Gently combine all the ingredients in a bowl. Serve with lamb, chicken, or fish.

128 calories; 5 g protein; 22 g carb; 4 g fat; 1 g saturated fat; 2 mg cholesterol; 6 g fiber; 239 mg sodium

The bulgur can be replaced with cooked quinoa or couscous.

Beets, Cannellini Beans and Goat Cheese

This salad is a great staple, but I encourage you to play around with the ingredients, depending on what is in season. It makes a lovely accompaniment to grilled, barbecued, or roasted meats.

Serves 4 | Prep time: 15 minutes, plus soaking time | Cooking time: 1 hour

1 cup dried cannellini beans or chickpeas
4 cups chicken stock
10 to 12 baby beets, trimmed and scrubbed, leaving ½-inch stalks
¼ cup walnut halves
¼ cup soft goat cheese marinated in olive oil
6 cups arugula

VINAIGRETTE
¼ cup extra virgin olive oil
1 tablespoon white wine vinegar or balsamic vinegar
1 tablespoon lemon juice
1 teaspoon Dijon mustard

Soak the beans in water overnight. Drain, then place them in a large saucepan and cover with stock. Bring to a boil, then reduce the heat and simmer for 1 hour or until tender. Drain.

Meanwhile, steam the beets for 5 to 8 minutes or until cooked through. Allow to cool slightly, then cut in half vertically. (Use kitchen gloves to avoid staining your hands red.)

To make the vinaigrette, place all the ingredients in a glass jar with a lid and shake well.

Combine the beans, beets, walnuts, goat cheese, and arugula in a bowl, pour the vinaigrette over the top, and gently toss.

407 calories; 13 g protein; 41 g carb; 22 g fat; 3 g saturated fat; 7 mg cholesterol; 12 g fiber; 536 mg sodium

Use feta marinated in olive oil instead of goat cheese, if preferred. Or toss in some sesame and sunflower seeds or, if you've made a batch, some caramelized walnuts (page 140).

Roasted Peppers, Marinated Artichokes and Parmesan

>

A versatile dish, this is great on an antipasto platter or served as a side with beef, lamb, fish, chicken, or turkey.

Serves 4 | Prep time: 10 minutes | Cooking time: 30 minutes

2 red bell peppers
6 artichokes marinated in olive oil, each cut into 4 segments
½ cup roughly chopped flat-leaf parsley
2 tablespoons shaved Parmesan

Preheat the oven to 425°F and line a 9 × 13-inch baking pan with parchment paper.

Cut the peppers in half lengthwise and remove the seeds, stem, and membrane. Place the peppers, cut-side down, on the baking pan and bake for 20 to 25 minutes or until they are blackened and blistered. Place them in a plastic bag for about 10 minutes.

Meanwhile, combine the artichokes, parsley, and Parmesan in a bowl.

Remove the peppers from the bag and peel off the skin. Slice into strips and combine with the artichoke mixture. Serve at room temperature.

180 calories; 3 g protein; 11 g carb; 14 g fat; 2 g saturated fat; 2 mg cholesterol; 3 g fiber; 320 mg sodium

For this recipe, look for whole artichoke hearts. If you can't find them, quartered artichokes marinated in oil are fine—just make sure you drain them well before use.

≡ Add a rinsed and drained can of chickpeas, lentils, or cannellini beans to the salad, if you like.

Fennel, Oranges, and Caramelized Walnuts

SERVES 6 TO 8
Prep time: 15 minutes
Cooking time: 5 minutes

1 fennel bulb, cut in half lengthwise
    and finely sliced
1 cup flat-leaf parsley leaves
2 tablespoons lemon juice
1 tablespoon extra virgin olive oil or
    lemon olive oil
Flaky sea salt and freshly ground
    black pepper to taste
2 oranges, skin and pith removed,
    sliced into rounds
10 to 12 cups mixed lettuce leaves
    (such as frisee, arugula, and butter
    lettuce)
Pomegranate and Orange Dressing
    (page 150)
Pomegranate seeds, optional

CARAMELIZED WALNUTS

1 tablespoon olive oil
1 tablespoon pure maple syrup (or use
    apple or pear juice concentrate)
1 cup walnut halves
Flaky sea salt

---

267 calories; 4 g protein; 17 g carb; 23 g fat; 1 g saturated fat; 0 mg cholesterol; 4 g fiber; 183 mg sodium

The recipe for caramelized walnuts makes a bit more than you'll need for this dish but you'll easily find a home for the leftovers. They're delicious sprinkled over any type of salad, and are particularly good with cheese, pears, and apples.

To make the caramelized walnuts, heat the oil and maple syrup in a nonstick frying pan over medium-high heat. Add the walnuts, toss well to coat, and cook for 2 to 3 minutes. Remove from the heat and sprinkle with sea salt. Transfer to a plate and cool, then refrigerate until needed.

Combine the fennel, parsley, lemon juice, olive oil, salt, and pepper in a large bowl, then cover and refrigerate if you have time. When ready to serve, add the orange slices, lettuce, and dressing to the fennel mixture and gently toss together. Transfer to a large, shallow serving bowl.

Sprinkle ½ cup caramelized walnuts and some pomegranate seeds, if using, over the salad. Serve with fish, chicken, lamb, or veal.

I always bake a large quantity of the caramelized walnuts and store them in a glass jar in the fridge, ready for salads, cheese platters, or after-dinner snacks with a little dark chocolate. Crumbling the nuts over the salad will make them go further.

Pecans may be used as well as or instead of the walnuts.

≡ If you like, add a handful of watercress, arugula, or baby spinach.

< Snow Pea, Avocado and Orange Salad

This vivid salad is a great side dish for kids, and is made with ingredients that are always readily available.

Serves 4 | Prep time: 15 minutes

12 ounces snow peas and/or sugar snap peas, topped and tailed, strings removed
1 avocado, cut in half lengthwise, then sliced into long segments
1 large orange, skin and pith removed, cut into segments
½ English cucumber, peeled, cut in half lengthwise, seeded, and sliced on the diagonal
Good squeeze of lemon juice
Olive oil, for drizzling
Toasted sesame seeds or cashews

Place the peas in a glass or ceramic bowl and cover with boiling water. Leave for 2 minutes then plunge into iced water to refresh. Transfer the snow peas to a serving bowl and gently combine with the remaining ingredients. Garnish with sesame seeds or cashews and serve with fish, chicken, or turkey.

---

163 calories; 3 g protein; 14 g carb; 12 g fat; 1 g saturated fat; 0 mg cholesterol; 5 g fiber; 11 mg sodium

Give this salad an Asian dimension by adding basil, mint, cilantro, a little sliced chile, soy sauce, and lemon or lime juice.

Broccoli with Lemon Olive Oil and Parmesan

Broccoli is rich in vitamins and, like cauliflower, Brussels sprouts, and cabbage, contains indoles, which may protect against cancer. Broccolini can also be used in this simple, flavorful dish.

Serves 4 | Prep time: 5 minutes | Cooking time: 5 minutes

1 pound broccoli, cut into florets
1 tablespoon lemon olive oil
1 tablespoon shaved or shredded Parmesan

Steam the broccoli for 3 to 4 minutes.

Heat the oil in a nonstick frying pan over medium-high heat. Add the broccoli and toss to coat in the oil. Cook for 1 minute, then add the Parmesan and toss to combine. Serve with fish, chicken, or veal.

---

68 calories; 4 g protein; 6 g carb; 4 g fat; 0 g saturated fat; 1 mg cholesterol; 3 g fiber; 54 mg sodium

Cauliflower or Brussels sprouts may be used instead of broccoli. If using sprouts, cut them in half and steam for 5 to 8 minutes or until tender. Add 1 tablespoon toasted pine nuts or almond slivers for extra crunch.

Buttered Cabbage

This simple vegetable dish is wonderful with meat and chicken dishes, especially Poached Ginger Chicken (page 101). It may be pureed if you prefer a smoother texture.

Serves 4 | Prep time: 10 minutes | Cooking time: 25 minutes

1½ tablespoons butter
½ head savoy or Chinese cabbage (about 1¼ pounds), core removed and finely sliced
1 cup chicken stock
Flaky sea salt to taste

Melt the butter in a large heavy-bottomed saucepan over medium heat. When foaming, add the cabbage and cook for 4 to 5 minutes, stirring well.

Pour in the stock, then reduce the heat and simmer, covered, for about 10 minutes. Remove the lid and cook for another 5 to 10 minutes, or until cooked to your liking. Season with salt. Serve as a bed for chicken, fish, pork, or turkey.

---

89 calories; 4 g protein; 10 g carb; 5 g fat; 3 g saturated fat; 14 mg cholesterol; 5 g fiber; 250 mg sodium

For extra flavor, add some chopped bacon or a tablespoon of fennel seeds to the butter. If cholesterol is a problem, use 1 tablespoon olive oil spread instead of the butter.

Cauliflower Bake   >

In my household, this delicious bake used to be mistaken for baked mashed potatoes and happily devoured by unsuspecting palates. Now they accept it as cauliflower "puff"!

Serves 4 | Prep time: 15 minutes | Cooking time: 35 minutes

1½ pounds cauliflower, roughly chopped
2 cups chicken stock or water
2 large eggs
2 teaspoons mayonnaise
Olive oil spray
¼ cup shredded Parmesan or grated mozzarella
1 tablespoon thyme leaves, optional

Preheat the oven to 400°F.

Place the cauliflower and stock in a medium saucepan over medium-high heat. Bring to a boil, then cover and cook for 10 minutes until soft. Strain and place the cauliflower in a bowl. Add the eggs and mayonnaise and puree with an immersion blender (or transfer to a blender).

Spray a small baking dish with oil and spoon in the cauliflower puree. Sprinkle with cheese and thyme, if using, and bake for 20 to 25 minutes or until golden. Serve with chicken, veal, beef, or lamb.

---

136 calories; 10 g protein; 10 g carb; 7 g fat; 2 g saturated fat; 115 mg cholesterol; 4 g fiber; 261 mg sodium

Celeriac and Roasted Sweet Potato Mash

Sweet potato is a delicious low-GI vegetable. Combining it with celeriac reduces the carb density and boosts the levels of antioxidants and vitamins. The mash makes a great accompaniment to just about everything, and kids love the chips or fries (see variation).

Serves 6 to 8 | Prep time: 15 minutes | Cooking time: 1 hour

2 sweet potatoes (about 1 pound each)
1 large celeriac (about 1¼ pounds), roughly cut into chunks
3 tablespoons chicken stock
1 tablespoon pure maple syrup, or pear or apple juice concentrate, optional
Flaky sea salt and freshly ground black pepper to taste

Preheat the oven to 400°F. Place the whole sweet potatoes directly on the rack and bake for 1 hour or until soft to touch. Remove from the oven. When cool enough to handle, cut in half lengthwise and scoop out the flesh.

Meanwhile, steam the celeriac until soft.

Blend or process the celeriac and sweet potato, then add the stock, maple syrup, if using, and salt and pepper. Mix well.

218 calories; 4 g protein; 50 g carb; 1 g fat; 0 g saturated fat; 0 mg cholesterol; 7 g fiber; 203 mg sodium

Sweet potato and celeriac chips or fries are a great alternative. Preheat the oven to 350°F and line a baking sheet with parchment paper. Cut 2 sweet potatoes and 1 small celeriac into ⅛-inch-thick slices for the chips or 2-inch matchsticks for the fries. Put them in a plastic bag with 2 tablespoons olive oil and a little salt and chopped rosemary and shake well. Place the slices on the sheet in a single layer and bake for 30 to 35 minutes or until crisp at the edges.

Baked Jerusalem Artichoke Chips with Parmesan and Garlic

Try these once and I'm sure you'll agree they are deliciously addictive. A word of caution, though— Jerusalem artichokes can cause severe gas if eaten in large quantities, so enjoy them in moderation.

Serves 6 | Prep time: 15 minutes | Cooking time: 1 hour

20 Jerusalem artichokes (about 1 pound)
2 tablespoons olive oil
2 to 4 garlic cloves, finely chopped (depending on your love of garlic!)
¼ cup shredded Parmesan

Preheat the oven to 400°F and line a large baking sheet with parchment paper.

Scrub the Jerusalem artichokes, pat dry, and cut into ⅛-inch-thick slices. Put them in a plastic bag with the oil, garlic, and Parmesan and shake well.

Place the slices on the sheet in a single layer and bake for 1 hour or until crisp at the edges. Serve with grilled meats or fish.

125 calories; 4 g protein; 15 g carb; 6 g fat; 1 g saturated fat; 3 mg cholesterol; 1 g fiber; 81 mg sodium

When Jerusalem artichokes are out of season, use sweet potatoes or carrots instead. Reduce the oven temperature to 350°F and bake for 30 to 35 minutes or until golden.

≡ Add a handful of chopped herbs to the bag—try rosemary, marjoram, or thyme.

Cauliflower and White Bean Puree

This comes close to being the ultimate comfort food for me, and I don't have to feel guilty about it! The beans increase the carb content but they are low GI and full of fiber and protein.

Serves 4 to 6 | Prep time: 15 minutes | Cooking time: 10 minutes

1½ pounds cauliflower, roughly chopped
One 15-ounce can cannellini beans, rinsed and drained
¾ cup roughly chopped flat-leaf parsley
2 teaspoons butter
Flaky sea salt and freshly ground black pepper to taste
2 garlic cloves, finely chopped
Chicken stock or water, optional

Steam the cauliflower for about 10 minutes until very soft. Transfer to a large saucepan, add the beans, parsley, and butter, and puree with an immersion blender, or process in a food processor until smooth. Season with salt and pepper and stir in the garlic. Add a little stock if you prefer a runnier consistency. Serve with grilled or barbecued meat, chicken, or fish.

---

156 calories; 8 g protein; 26 g carb; 3 g fat; 1 g saturated fat; 5 mg cholesterol; 9 g fiber; 414 mg sodium

Halve the quantity of cauliflower and replace with ¼ head savoy cabbage or half a large celeriac, steamed with the cauliflower. If you like, stir in 2 tablespoons low-fat cream cheese for a creamier texture.

Shredded Celeriac with Fennel Seeds

I love celeriac and always miss it when it's not available during the summer months. The addition of fennel seeds makes this dish particularly "more-ish."

Serves 2 | Prep time: 10 minutes | Cooking time: 15 minutes

2 teaspoons olive oil
1 tablespoon fennel seeds
½ celeriac, shredded (about 12 ounces)
¼ cup chicken stock
Flaky sea salt and freshly ground black pepper to taste

Heat the oil in a medium saucepan over medium heat, add the fennel seeds and cook, covered, for 10 to 20 seconds. Add the celeriac and cook for a few minutes, then stir in the stock.

Reduce the heat to low and cook, covered, for another 10 minutes. Season with salt and pepper. Serve with chicken, fish, lamb, or beef—any simple protein dish.

---

128 calories; 3 g protein; 18 g carb; 6 g fat; 0 g saturated fat; 1 mg cholesterol; 4 g fiber; 423 mg sodium

The prep time will be reduced if you use a food processor to prepare the celeriac, but it will add to your washing-up time! I prefer to use a handheld shredder.

For a slightly creamier dish, add 1 teaspoon white wine vinegar and 2 teaspoons low-fat sour cream when you add the stock.

Puy-Style Lentils with Orange and Sage

Puy-style lentils do not require soaking and retain a firm texture when cooked, making them perfect for salads and side dishes. They are available at natural food stores and many supermarkets. If you can't find them, regular brown lentils will do, though they take a little longer to cook.

Serves 4 | Prep time: 15 minutes | Cooking time: 1 hour

1 tablespoon olive oil
1 onion, finely chopped
1 carrot, grated or finely chopped
2 celery stalks, finely chopped
1½ cups chicken stock
½ cup puy-style lentils
1 tablespoon finely chopped sage
Grated zest of 1 large orange
½ cup fresh orange juice
2 garlic cloves, finely chopped

Heat the oil in a large heavy-bottomed saucepan or Dutch oven over medium-high heat. Add the onion, carrot, and celery and cook for 5 minutes, stirring regularly (add a little stock if the vegetables start to stick). Stir in the lentils and sage and cook for another minute.

Pour in the remaining stock, orange zest, and juice and simmer, covered, for 45 minutes, stirring every 10 minutes or so. Add a little more stock if the lentils start to stick. Stir in the garlic and cook for another 5 minutes. Serve with turkey, pork, chicken, or fish (it's particularly good with salmon).

157 calories; 8 g protein; 23 g carb; 4 g fat; 0 g saturated fat; 2 mg cholesterol; 9 g fiber; 62 mg sodium

If preferred, use well-rinsed quinoa instead of the lentils. This will greatly reduce your cooking time. Cook the vegetables for 8 to 10 minutes, then add the quinoa and sage. Stir for 1 minute, then add the remaining ingredients and simmer, covered, for 10 to 15 minutes.

Warm Eggplant and Red Pepper Salsa

The combination of eggplant, onion, red bell pepper, and zucchini is well loved in Mediterranean cooking. Here, I've brought these colorful ingredients together in a warm salsa that goes well with lamb, chicken, and fish.

Serves 4 | Prep time: 20 minutes, plus standing time | Cooking time: 25 minutes

Table salt, for sprinkling
1 large eggplant, cut into ½-inch cubes
2 tablespoons olive oil
1 red onion, cut into ½-inch squares
1½ celery stalks, cut into ½-inch pieces
1 red bell pepper, cut into ½-inch squares
1 zucchini, cut into ½-inch cubes
2 garlic cloves, finely chopped
One 15-ounce can chickpeas or cannellini beans, rinsed and drained
¾ cup mint, leaves torn
3 tablespoons pine nuts, lightly toasted

Lightly salt the eggplant and set aside for 15 minutes, then rinse and drain on paper towels, pressing gently to remove as much liquid as possible.

Heat 1 tablespoon of the oil in a large heavy-bottomed saucepan or frying pan over medium-high heat and cook the onion, celery, red pepper, zucchini, and garlic for 7 to 8 minutes.

Heat the remaining oil in a separate nonstick frying pan over medium-high heat and cook the eggplant for 5 minutes or until golden and cooked through, shaking the pan regularly.

Gently add the eggplant, chickpeas, and mint to the red pepper and zucchini mixture and cook for another 5 to 10 minutes. Sprinkle with the pine nuts just before serving.

277 calories; 11 g protein; 35 g carb; 12 g fat; 1 g saturated fat; 0 mg cholesterol; 11g fiber; 324 mg sodium

Quinoa, Roasted Sweet Potato and Pomegranate

SERVES 6

Prep time: 15 minutes
Cooking time: 50 minutes

1 pound sweet potatoes, cut into
    ¾-inch cubes
Olive oil spray
Fresh orange juice, for drizzling
Flaky sea salt to taste
1 cup quinoa
2 cups chicken stock or water
1 red onion, finely sliced
1½ cups flat-leaf parsley leaves
¾ cup cilantro
2 cups arugula
½ cup pomegranate seeds
Grated zest of 1 orange

POMEGRANATE AND
ORANGE DRESSING
3 tablespoons extra virgin olive oil
2 tablespoons white wine vinegar
1 tablespoon pomegranate molasses
2 tablespoons fresh orange juice

---

299 calories; 7 g protein; 45 g carb; 10 g
fat; 0 g saturated fat; 2 mg cholesterol; 11 g
fiber; 135 mg sodium

Quinoa is a delicious, low-GI grain that may be used instead of rice, bulgur, or couscous. Its flavor really shines in this pretty salad.

Preheat the oven to 350°F and line a baking sheet with parchment paper.

Place the sweet potatoes on the sheet in a single layer, then spray with oil, drizzle with a little orange juice, and sprinkle with salt. Bake for 40 to 50 minutes.

Meanwhile, rinse the quinoa thoroughly, then place in a medium saucepan. Add the stock or water and bring to a boil, then reduce the heat and simmer, covered, for 10 minutes until the quinoa is tender and translucent. Drain.

To make the dressing, place all ingredients in a glass jar with a lid and shake well.

Combine the sweet potatoes, quinoa, onion, parsley, cilantro, arugula, pomegranate seeds, and orange zest in a large bowl and toss well. Drizzle with the dressing and toss again. Serve with lamb, beef, chicken, or fish.

This dressing is wonderful on just about any type of salad, even the simplest bowl of lettuce leaves.

Sauteed Mushrooms and Spinach

This is delicious served with most types of protein for breakfast, lunch, or dinner! Try it spooned over low-GI toast with a little crumbled goat cheese or feta.

Serves 4 | Prep time: 10 minutes | Cooking time: 20 minutes

1 tablespoon olive oil (or use 1½ tablespoons butter)
2 garlic cloves, finely chopped
1 pound cremini mushrooms or white mushrooms, sliced
½ cup roughly chopped flat-leaf parsley
½ cup chicken stock
12 cups baby spinach

Heat the oil in a large nonstick frying pan over medium heat. When sizzling, add the garlic, mushrooms, and parsley and cook, stirring, for 2 to 3 minutes. Pour in the stock, then reduce the heat to low and cook for another 10 minutes. Add the spinach and cook, covered, for 3 to 4 minutes until wilted.

---

92 calories; 5 g protein; 13 g carb; 4 g fat; 0 g saturated fat; 1 mg cholesterol; 5 g fiber; 136 mg sodium

Use whatever fresh herbs you have on hand—I often add thyme instead of parsley.

Cannellini Beans and Spinach with Garlic and Basil >

This versatile recipe is great with or without the spinach. Serve it as a side dish with chicken, lamb, or veal, or pile it onto toasted low-GI bread, sprinkle with mozzarella, and lightly grill until the cheese has melted.

Serves 4 | Prep time: 10 minutes | Cooking time: 25 minutes

1 tablespoon olive oil
1 onion, finely chopped
One 15-ounce can cannellini beans, rinsed and drained
One 14.5-ounce can crushed tomatoes
6 cups baby spinach
2 garlic cloves, finely chopped
½ cup finely chopped basil

Heat the oil in a medium saucepan over medium-high heat and cook the onion for 4 to 5 minutes until softened and lightly golden. Add the beans and crushed tomatoes, then reduce the heat and simmer for 10 minutes. Add the spinach, a handful at a time, and gently fold into the bean mixture until wilted. Stir in the garlic and basil and cook for another 5 minutes.

---

181 calories; 8 g protein; 30 g carb; 4 g fat; 0 g saturated fat; 0 mg cholesterol; 9 g fiber; 428 mg sodium

This is delicious baked in red or green bell peppers. Simply cut the tops off the peppers (keep for later), place on a baking sheet, and bake in a preheated 350°F oven for 15 minutes. Remove from the oven and fill with the mixture. Sprinkle with some grated pecorino or mozzarella, put the pepper tops on the sheet, and bake for another 15 minutes.

≡ Vary the flavor by adding 12 sliced olives, a couple of roughly chopped artichokes, or 2 tablespoons capers.

Sweets

Occasionally it's nice to finish a meal with a little sweet something. Fruit forms the basis of most of my desserts, and I like to enhance its natural sweetness with spices, nuts, and a touch of maple syrup. It's no secret that dark chocolate offers many health benefits when eaten in moderation, so try the Almond, Ginger, and Dark Chocolate Bites—they don't last long in our household!

Poached Pears in Honey and Orange Syrup with Cinnamon Cream

SERVES 6
Prep time: 10 minutes
Cooking time: 15 minutes

CINNAMON CREAM
½ cup heavy cream
½ teaspoon ground cinnamon

3 tablespoons verjuice or white wine
Grated zest and juice of 1 orange
Good pinch of saffron
6 to 8 pears, peeled, cored, and
    quartered
2 tablespoons honey

198 calories; 1 g protein; 33 g carb; 8 g fat;
5 g saturated fat; 27 mg cholesterol; 4 g
fiber; 8 mg sodium

Fragrant pears in season are one of my favorite fruits. Here, I've cut them into quarters, but you can also leave them whole—just add another 10 minutes or so to the cooking time.

To make the cinnamon cream, whisk together the cream and cinnamon until thick. Refrigerate until ready to serve.

Combine all the remaining ingredients and ½ cup hot water in a heavy-bottomed saucepan. Bring to a boil, then reduce the heat and simmer, covered, for 10 minutes. Remove the pears and boil the syrup for 1 to 2 minutes or until the liquid has reduced by about a third.

To serve, ladle the fruit and syrup into small bowls and dollop with a little cinnamon cream.

You could also use maple syrup for this, but the honey and saffron are great together.

Use low-fat plain yogurt instead of cream if you are watching your fat intake.

High Protein, Low GI, Bold Flavor

< Slow-Baked Apples with Vanilla Yogurt Cream

Baked apples with cinnamon is a favorite standby when I need a little comfort food. This recipe works with both red and green apples—use whatever looks fresh and good on the day.

Serves 4 | Prep time: 10 minutes | Cooking time: 30 minutes

4 apples, cored and cut horizontally into ¾-inch-thick slices
½ teaspoon ground cinnamon
Macadamia nut oil or olive oil, for brushing
1 tablespoon pear or apple juice concentrate

VANILLA YOGURT CREAM
3 tablespoons low-fat cream cheese
3 tablespoons low-fat plain yogurt
1 tablespoon pear or apple juice concentrate, or pure maple syrup
1 teaspoon vanilla extract

Preheat the oven to 350°F and line a baking sheet with parchment paper.

Place the apple slices in a plastic bag, add the cinnamon, and shake well to coat. Arrange the apples on the sheet in a single layer, brush with oil and pear juice concentrate, and bake for 30 minutes or until the apple slices are cooked through.

Meanwhile, to make the vanilla yogurt cream, blend all the ingredients together.

To serve, arrange the apple slices on a plate and drizzle with the yogurt cream.

---

133 calories; 2 g protein; 23 g carb; 4 g fat; 2 g saturated fat; 8 mg cholesterol; 4 g fiber; 50 mg sodium

Enhance the yogurt cream with extra flavorings, such as a few tablespoons of dried currants or finely chopped dried apricots, some grated ginger, or a little lemon zest. Sprinkle with crushed toasted almonds.

Orange, Grape and Pomegranate Salad with Mint Syrup

This light, fresh concoction will cleanse your palate while satisfying your post-dinner cravings for something sweet.

Serves 4 | Prep time: 15 minutes, plus cooling time | Cooking time: 5 minutes

1 pomegranate
4 oranges, skin and pith removed, cut into slices then quartered
8 ounces red or green grapes, cut in half

MINT SYRUP
1 tablespoon pear or apple juice concentrate
¼ cup finely chopped mint

To make the mint syrup, place the pear juice concentrate, half the mint, and ¼ cup water in a small saucepan over high heat. Bring to a boil, then remove the pan from the heat. Pour the syrup into a pitcher and refrigerate until nicely chilled.

Meanwhile, roll the pomegranate firmly on a chopping board, then cut it in half. Place the halves over a glass bowl and tap the skin to dislodge the seeds. Turn them inside out to remove any remaining seeds and juices. Add the orange slices and grapes and refrigerate until ready to serve.

Strain the cooled syrup, discarding the mint, then pour it over the fruit. Add the remaining fresh mint and toss gently to combine. Serve in glass dishes to show off the lovely colors.

---

134 calories; 2 g protein; 34 g carb; 1 g fat; 0 g saturated fat; 0 mg cholesterol; 4 g fiber; 4 mg sodium

Use strawberries, blueberries, or raspberries when pomegranates are out of season. This is also great with large mandarins and blueberries for a wonderful display of colors and textures.

Add 1 teaspoon pomegranate molasses or rose or mint water to the mint syrup instead of the pear juice concentrate.

Tahini, Fig and Maple Syrup Balls

Tahini is made from hulled, stone-ground sesame seeds. It is probably best known as a key ingredient in hummus, but it is also often used in desserts.

Makes about 24 | Prep time: 15 minutes

½ cup tahini
5 dried figs, finely chopped
5 pieces crystallized ginger, finely chopped
3 tablespoons LSA (page 13)
3 tablespoons sesame seeds
3 tablespoons pepitas
3 tablespoons dried currants
3 tablespoons old-fashioned oats
3 tablespoons unsweetened shredded or flaked coconut
2 tablespoons pure maple syrup

Line a baking sheet with parchment paper.

Place all the ingredients in a bowl and mix together well. Roll the mixture into walnut-sized balls, place them on the baking sheet, and refrigerate until firm.

96 calories; 3 g protein; 9 g carb; 6 g fat; 2 g saturated fat; 0 mg cholesterol; 2 g fiber; 6 mg sodium

The dried fruit and maple syrup do increase the carbs, but the fiber and fat of the seeds, tahini, and oats reduce the GI index of the balls, so they are nutritiously dense.

Add crushed toasted almonds or other low-GI dried fruits, such as chopped dried apricots or goji berries.

Almond, Ginger and Dark Chocolate Bites >

If ginger is not your thing, replace it with finely chopped dried fruit, such as cranberries, figs, apricots, or goji berries. Loaded with vitamin C and antioxidants, goji are a food to enjoy!

Makes about 15 | Prep time: 10 minutes | Cooking time: 10 minutes

4 ounces slivered almonds
2 ounces dark chocolate (70 percent cocoa)
¼ cup crystallized ginger pieces, finely chopped

Place the almonds in a nonstick frying pan and cook over medium heat for 3 to 4 minutes or until golden, tossing constantly. Remove and set aside to cool.

Place the chocolate in a heatproof bowl and set over a saucepan of barely simmering water (don't let the bowl touch the water). Simmer very gently for 2 to 3 minutes or until the chocolate has melted. Add the almonds and ginger to the chocolate and mix well.

Line a baking sheet with parchment paper. Spoon heaped teaspoons of the chocolate mixture onto the sheet, then place in the fridge until the "bites" are firm.

75 calories; 2 g protein; 7 g carb; 5 g fat; 1 g saturated fat; 0 mg cholesterol; 1 g fiber; 2 mg sodium

For a more refined look, pour a little melted chocolate onto a baking sheet lined with parchment paper (each chocolate round should have a diameter of about 1 inch). Drop your choice of chopped ingredients into the chocolate and refrigerate until solid (fresh cherries dipped in chocolate are particularly delicious!). Store in the fridge if there are any left to store!

If you like, sprinkle the bites with roasted shredded coconut, or add some sunflower or pumpkin seeds to the mixture.

Acknowledgments

A special thank-you to my husband, Greg, for his encouragement and thoughtful, constructive criticism, and to our children, Jackson, Olivia, and Georgia, for their adolescent honesty.

To my gorgeous and faithful friends Ciara, Megan, Melissa, Pix, and Toni for their support, creativity, and passion for great food.

Thank you to the team behind the original edition at Penguin Australia: publisher Julie Gibbs, managing editor Ingrid Ohlsson, designers Evi Oetomo and Nikki Townsend, and design coordinator Megan Piggot. A very special thank-you to my wonderful editor Rachel Carter, whose clever and gentle guidance made the most tedious of jobs a joy.

Thank you to Dr. Jennie Brand-Miller for her foreword to the North American edition, and for her work on the glycemic index, which has been a valuable source of information and inspiration.

Finally, sincere thanks to Simon Griffiths for his eagle eye and beautiful photographs, and to the fabulous "Fi Team": stylists Fiona Hammond and Fiona Rigg for their wonderful work and advice at the shoot.

Index